TOMORROW'S WORLD ORDER

[TWO]

THE

CONSTITUTION

&

OUR

IMPORTANT

PRINCIPLES

By

David Gomadza

Founder and President

Tomorrow's World Order

DEDICATION

We have the only method and system capable of increasing individual, national and global wealth to levels never seen before. We aim to eradicate all global problems by introducing a completely new system of governance and fiscal planning and management. The current system is obsolete and only our system is the answer. Are you ready? I am and we are!!

David Gomadza

TABLE OF CONTENTS

ACKNOWLEDGMENTS

vii

A big thank you to all those who supported and believed in us.
A New World Order.
A New Chapter in Mankind's History.

PART 1

1. PREAMBLE

We as [Tomorrow's World Order] abbreviated as TWO; We intend to register on the Great Britain register with the intention to contest elections in all England, Scotland, and Wales (Great Britain register).

I as the Global Party Officer/ Party Leader [David Gomadza] declare that

[Tomorrow's World Order] party intends to contest elections in UK parliamentary general elections all England, Scotland, and Wales.

Through our constitution and the adopted Financial Scheme of [Tomorrow's World Order], the party has processes in place to comply with the rules that govern the election and financial activities of our party. Find our constitution below and the attached Financial Scheme that our party [Tomorrow's World Order] has adopted. In all our dealings within the United Kingdom and globally we confirm that our constitution and how Tomorrow's World Order as a party operates, adhere to all principles of full equality and comply with the Equality and Human Rights Commission rules, laws and regulations. For clarity, any reference to masculine in this constitution can be a reference to any; either feminine or masculine. We as Tomorrow World Order [UK] declare that as a political party to be established in the United Kingdom, we shall observe the rules and regulations in our conduct as a political party as stated in the Political Party, Election and Referendum Act 2000.

Our party TWO [UK] shall act fair and not favor people due to their religious beliefs, sex, race, education, other beliefs, ethnic origin, class, sexual orientation, etc. the list is not exhaustive. We as TWO [UK] in conducting all our activities shall observe the requirements placed upon us by the United Kingdom of observing the rule of law, democracy, liberty and all human rights.

2. OBJECTIVES OF TOMORROW'S WORLD ORDER [GLOBAL] AND TOMORROW'S WORLD ORDER [UK]

To introduce a new system of governance both at a local and global scale that emphasizes the printing of new money as the only true source of growth and individual, national and global wealth.

To introduce a global leader who is not biased; a leader that represents all mankind and one who is for the people globally, one to lead all nations acting as an overseer and the guiding force with the aim of taking humanity out of the defensive stages where weapons and defense take center stage.

To ban global wars, weapons manufacturing, possession, and trading.

To ban the killings of innocent women and children globally.

To ban sanctions that affect the voiceless; women and children.

To shift the thinking from austerity: living within your means, to an emphasis on growth giving the people more power in decisions and policies that affect them.

To bring to all mankind wealth levels never experienced before.

To protect already accumulated wealth and put things in place to make sure that this wealth is passed on from generation to generation rather than be taken by the government or institutions or charities.

To protect savings already accumulated and put things in place so that these savings often accumulated over the years won't be lost in a short period of time.

To introduce a health plan that is free but fair where all citizens have to maintain a balance in their government-owned-yet-individual savings account above a certain level to qualify for free health, with the government using this savings account as collateral to offer free service. The government depending on circumstances can match the balance, double it, triple it or even multiple this tenfold in order to provide enough cover.

To introduce a new government-backing of its citizens where it is indebted to its people where it bails-out the people instead of banks first, a system where governments are mandated to protect the wealth of its citizens and are proactive to cushion the wealth by providing loans, mortgages, etc. through the individual savings-yet-government held account. Instead of collecting taxes and national insurance from income and wages the government shall collect savings straight to the citizen's savings account which the government will use to assess eligibility levels for free health, loans, mortgages and pension support, the account remains in possession of the government until such a time when the individual reaches a certain age say 60 to have access to it and or if the contribution balance reaches a certain value e.g. $10 000 for argument's sake then the person can have access to it.

To abolish the taking of wealth of the deceased-without-relatives by the government,

To ban donations of wealth especially by the elderly to government, institutions like hospitals and or charities. Wealth to be left to relatives only and even distant relatives rather than the government, institutions like hospitals and or charities.

To abolish income tax payments and collection by the government.

To ban payments of national insurance and collection of these by the government.

To introduce instead a collection from the income of a single-digit-figure initially and opening of an individual savings-but government-owned account. An account that will be held by the government until a time when a person reached a certain age, or the savings account balance reaches a certain amount before the person has access to it.

This individual savings-yet government-held account's balance will act as collateral in order for the government to offer free health, loans, mortgages, etc.

To advance and promote the printing of new money as the only true source of growth and wealth to a level never seen before.

To introduce a new system to deal with hyperinflation and all issues associated with the printing of new money.

To introduce a new system where all nations on earth must

adopt our digital currency as the New Single Reserve Global Currency [NSRGC] in order to take humanity to levels never seen before.

To advance a system where all nations on earth will use two currencies as the base currencies namely their own sovereign national currency as the first currency and secondly adopt and use our digital currency FutureGoldCoin as the second base currency, even though nations can use more than two currencies these must be the two critical currencies to achieve growth and wealth to levels never experienced before.

To advance and lay a new system and framework of global governance where there is the rule of law, democracy, peace and wealth for all to new heights. A system adhered to by all simply because the system represents everyone and is for all; an effective system.

To introduce a new system of analyzing debt and dealing with individual, national and global debt and a new system of treating debt as having a depreciation value.

To introduce a new system that encourages individual, national and global savings, introducing the government-owned yet individual savings accounts, introducing Tomorrow's World Order Global Reserve Bank where all nations after printing new money have to deposit this new money in the Global Reserve Bank as savings which we will treat as collateral and offer them the equivalent of our universal global digital currency the FutureGoldCoin which they must use in their economy to achieve growth to new heights.

To introduce a new system that will take humanity to the next stage of development away from the defensive stage in which we are stuck in; where mankind makes weapons-cheaper and then uses the weapons to get the expensive resources like oil.

To introduce a new system that will increase affordability to levels high enough to buy any resources be it oil etc. at market prices instead of relying on weapons to fetch these.

To introduce new laws and regulations to offer peace and consolation to those who seek justice and on the other hand, introduce a new universal justice system that is fair and effective and feared by all, regardless.

To maintain individual differences in people and nations brought by mother nature recognizing this as everyone's right by not insisting or imposing changes but maintaining individualism as long as the differences are within the law. That means preserving the nation-specific difference strengthening the borders of each nation as desired as long as all are willing to abide by all international laws and our rules and regulations. Encouraging diversity.

Above all, bringing peace to all mankind with the aim of networking and cooperating together on a global scale.

To achieve all this, we aim to appoint people who we will field-in in all democratic elections at all levels with the aim to win seats and office so that in the end our appointed and elected leaders become the rulers and leaders of the United Kingdom in all England, Scotland, and Wales and globally. Leaders from Tomorrow's World Order must bring wealth levels never experienced before, empower all and bring peace to all while improving life, quality of life and raising everyone's self-esteem to the levels never thought of the only way nature intended. Only Tomorrow's World Order has the answers.

PART 2

THE CONSTITUTION

TOMORROW'S WORLD ORDER

1. NAME OF THE PARTY

The name of this political organization shall be [Tomorrow's World Order] United Kingdom and [Tomorrow's World Order] Global hereafter referred to as TWO [UK] and TWO [Global].

TWO [UK] is a constituent country-specific part of Tomorrow's World Order [Global] and is subject to its rules and constitution.

Our slogan is; Your Future Your Say.

The geographic area of TWO [UK] is in all England, Scotland, and Wales.

2. FUNCTIONS AND OBJECTIVES OF THE PARTY

The first aim and the objective of Tomorrow's World Order is to endorse our selected candidates to contest, win and take roles as the Prime Minister or President through the Parliamentary elections or Presidential elections and to participate in the general elections; to be selected for roles in the House of Commons, the Senate and the House of the Representations depending on the country in question.

2.1 The aim of TWO [UK]

is to represent Tomorrow's World Order [global] in the United Kingdom that is in England, Scotland and Wales promoting its views and principles as in its constitution.

"The purpose of this organization shall be;
To contest elections and win positions and seats in all elections and at all levels of the government and one day to win the leadership contest so that our political party will be the ruling party in the United Kingdom that is in England, Scotland and Wales.

To write, develop, publicize and promote the views of Tomorrow's World Order [Global] in the United Kingdom that is in all England, Scotland and Wales and applying these on a national scale with the aim of taking humanity to another level of development bringing in wealth to all mankind at levels never seen before through our policies, procedures and rules. We as a people have the potential to achieve great yet we are operating below our optimal levels.

We aim to change mankind's thinking of emphasizing austerity measures and show all mankind that growth is the only way nature intended. Prosperity to all mankind and not just to the few privileged ones.

To plan, organize, promote and take part in all peaceful activities within the United Kingdom.

To advance our agendas and gain the trust, support, and backing of all the people and convince all that only our policies are the way forward. We have heard and seen all current policies in play and we already know the disappointment and now it's time for change and change can only mean growth and levels of wealth for all never experienced before. We have the answers.

We aim to participate in all elections and referendums at all levels,

We aim to take all won seats and where there is ambiguity the party leader must decide. If still doubt exist, the national party leader can put the matter before the global leader of Tomorrow's World Order unless it is the same person in which case he has, or she has to decide therein.

The elected members to represent our party at all levels and advance our goals and objectives. The national party for that region here TWO [UK] will link and cooperate with the main branch TWO [Global] and with other local institutions, bodies or even other charities, etc. for the sake of carrying out its duties as in the constitution or where the leader sees fit.

2.2 Powers of the TWO [UK] and TWO [Global] Political Parties;

To achieve our goals and objectives and within the framework of the law in carrying out our activities the party shall have powers to;
Fundraise and seek donations from anyone who qualifies as governed by the Political Parties Electoral Referendum Act 2000 and to accept those donations; recording these as stipulating by the governing body; keeping all records for reporting to the PPERA at the time we are required reporting.
To raise any contributions and receive these according to the rules and regulations.
To seek, accept and receive the fees in relation to the joining of our party and subscription fees and to register all those on our register who have shown interest and commitment to join us and be governed by our laws and regulations. A register of which we will keep and one that members will have an excess to, and one which others can request in writing to the membership secretary or anyone delegated at the time.
We as TWO [UK] have powers to publish materials in line with our aims and objectives which we will use for campaigning and for fulfilling our objectives. Material we can distribute free or for a fee, material we can publish in any format and to anyone around the globe and material which will contain our core values and principles, therefore, materials that belong to TWO [UK] and on behalf of TWO [Global].
We shall have powers to select and elect people through the party leader to various positions within our party and to employ and pay these people we see fit as they help in the running of the party as long as it is within the guiding principles of the laws of the country concerned and globally as a whole.
We as TWO [UK] and TWO [Global] have the power to open bank accounts for the sake of carrying out our activities and to purchase and make payments for infrastructure and other

consumables as long as everything is for the purpose of fulfilling our objectives as guided by the constitution. That means we can acquire and run, lease, rent and or sell buildings.

We have powers to take out insurances for the sake of carrying out our duties and to use the extra cash we might have accumulated to be put to good use through investing these in accordance with other applying laws e.g. the Trustee laws.

We can carry out any activities we see fit as long as they are according to law; to plan, to obtain services and resources we need, and this can mean entering into contracts to get real estate or personal property with the aim of fulfilling our objects. This can also mean us following the rules and regulations of the UK and other nation's Companies Acts as we will register our party as a Private Company limited by guarantee without share capital etc. as we see fit in order for the listed company to fund the party in perpetuity but the company having the funds secured without it paying out dividends to shareholders.

3 MEMBERSHIP REQUIREMENTS

This part deals with membership of the party. In short, anyone can join as long as they agree to be governed by this constitution and our values and declare and promise that they believe and relate to our values and objectives. This part explains the roles of all members and what is expected of them. As a general rule; members can resign in writing. Membership can be revoked due to several factors e.g. disregarding the constitution and other laws and acting in competition with the party etc. details below. Non-payment cannot result in cessation of membership as a Membership Payment Buffer account is to be set to cover non-payments. But non-payment for a year or more might make that membership be regarded as ended.

3.1 Putting things in place to ensure compliance with the constitution, bylaws and other laws.

For the sake of membership and employment everyone who becomes our member, and those employed by us will be considered as having fully declared their willingness and express agreement to be governed by our constitution and our party rules and express a willingness to follow other laws like the equality laws, [members can be asked to sign a document stating the above at initial registration or when taking up employment with TWO].

Not to do or be involved in acts that contradict what we stand for or what is regarding as breaking the laws of the UK and all nations we operate in. If it later comes to light that such a person has disregarded our constitution from the date the constitution comes into effect and thereafter and any rules and has been involved in acts that are against any laws of the UK and all other countries we are established such a person will automatically cease to become a member and or employee of TWO [UK] and TWO [Global] and the party leader of the country concerned or any delegated person will dismiss that individual from the party so as not to tarnish the party as long as the person can attend a meeting with party members before the dismissal for his or her case to be heard, where he can attend with a friend, and a member of TWO be provided to be on his side and any appeals to be lodged within four weeks.

3.2 Rules on membership of [Tomorrow's World Order].

The general body of TWO [UK] shall be composed of all members in the United Kingdom including all England, Scotland, and Wales who have joined, registered and paid the joining fee or subscription fee and whose accounts are up to date having paid all monthly or annual fees, etc. and all new who intend to register and or are in the process of joining.

Membership is open to all regardless of age, sex, race, color, sex, creed, gender identity, sexual orientation,

disability, socioeconomic status, national origin, etc. This list is not exhaustive.

A member here is anyone;

willing to advance our aims and become part of this great movement,

willing to follow and abide by the rules of TWO [UK] and its constitution,

willing to pay the joining fee and or the subscription irrespective of their previous political affiliation as long as they declare that on becoming a member this is the only party they will belong to thereafter.

Membership starts when the correct fee has been paid and the person registered in the electronic or physical register.

The members will be responsible for paying the annual membership fee to be decided at the first annual general meeting.

The membership secretary is responsible for maintaining and keeping the membership list. The party leader or secretary can appoint the membership secretary.

The leadership shall be made of a President of TWO [UK] who shall represent the political party with the aim of contesting in general elections and winning the leadership role to take the top office.

An active-member should not be;

Someone who has not paid fees for more than 3 months, [but non-payment cannot lead to cessation of membership the Membership Buffer Fund is to be used to pay-off what that

person owes],
Someone who is facing disciplinary that can lead to expulsion,
Someone who has joined another party that is way different
from the values we stand for e.g. a party that is restrictive and or
does not obey say equality laws, etc.
All members to have a registered email address or other
electronic or physical form e.g. correspondence address in order
to receive monthly updates and news about the party and to
participate fully in all activities regarding the party TWO
[UK].

3.3 The privileges and responsibilities of membership are;

To take part in the campaign and attend all meetings and if
elected to officers' roles to vote and participate fully in the
activities of the organization.
To acknowledge that any member will abide by the constitution
and our rules and to declare that they have no intention to act as
in conflict with the party and what we stand for.
To pay up monthly subscription fees and where a person has not
paid for a year and did not express the promise to pay will be
regarded as ceased being a member.
All members have duties to abide by the constitutions and our
rules
Any acts in conflict or contrary to what we stand for or
competition with other members and the party will lead a
member to disciplinary action.
Members who have not settled their subscription accounts have
no voting rights they are considered for the three months they
haven't settled as dormant members and as such have no rights
and powers to vote or be expected to choose new members but
can take part in all other party activities. Unless they made
other arrangements or promised to pay at a specific date which
must not be more than 30 days ahead.

3.4 Revocation of Membership.

Members can resign on their own but in writing to the membership secretary giving a two weeks' notice.
Membership may be revoked by Party leadership or any appointed party members delegated to do so due to;
acting in conflict with the party rules and constitution,
having breached our rules and regulations without any regard,
and carrying out activities that compete with the party and constitution,
and any disregard for the rules and laws of the country from the date the constitution comes into effect in that country, the list is not exhaustive.
The disciplinary policy means everyone must be heard as long as they appeal within four weeks and is entitled to a meeting where the party leader or the disciplinary committee or any appointed member can hear the case with the party leader informed and issuing the final decision. The individual concerned can choose to be accompanied by a friend or any member to be appointed by the party members responsible for the meeting. The person where the case is complicated can choose to appeal to the global leadership who will make the final decision. Their decision is final, and no further appeal is available after that. The leadership depending on circumstances can inform the person to rejoin after a certain period say minimum 3 months as long as the case was not very serious but the person if he or she had a party officer role and where there are issues of trust must not rejoin the management team but can be an ordinary member.

3.5 Creation of a Membership Buffer Account.

A Membership Buffer Account must be set up where funds are kept into this account to cover for those who still want to be members but can't pay the membership. Such people need to send their names to the membership secretary. No one shall leave the party due to the failure to pay membership fees. Anyone who has not paid for membership for three months will have their memberships paid from this account automatically.

But failure to pay for a year without pointing to financial difficulties can lead the membership secretary or committee to regard such a membership as ceased.

4 THE PARTY'S DECISION-MAKING PROCESS

This part deals with the party's decision-making process. The leader or President of the Tomorrow's World Order Global is the ultimate decision-making person, but he is answerable to the Ultimate Executive Power Board that also has powers to make, correct, suggest and recommended decisions. At a national level, the party leader or President is responsible for the overall decision-making process, but he is also answerable to a National Executive Power Board who acts to check, verify, recommend, liaise, suggest, etc. and work with this leader to make sure that the party objectives can be realized. The general quorum for meetings is seven. Annual general meetings are compulsory for all with special, and extraordinary meetings called upon when needed, etc. For all meetings, two weeks' notice is needed, and communication is in writing postal or electronic.

4.1 Role of the Ultimate Executive Power Party Leader

This is the highest office of Tomorrow's World Order. At the moment is held by the founder me [David Gomadza] and the Ultimate President of Tomorrow's World Order.

The Roles;

As the founder of the political party; laying down the fundamental principles and rules to be followed and to write down the constitution clearly stating the objectives of the party as a whole on a global scale.

To lay the foundation and basis and the core founding principles of Tomorrow's World Order.

I have the power to define the path the party will follow.

I am the authorizing authority for any amendments and any rectification or addition to the constitutions, rules, new systems, and procedures. Most of the changes require my signature as the leader unless I have delegated the task to another member until such a time when any Executive leader can do so.

Very active role in making sure that members take control and leadership in all nations on earth starting with the first seven nations, followed by the next 24 nations and then the 42 nations with the aim of putting members peacefully of course through

contesting in parliamentary elections globally in leadership roles in order to realize the plan of implementing a brand new system of global governance, fiscal monitoring, planning and management and the judiciary system.
I have tasks to invent, draft, design, put things in place, implement, monitor, and follow up to introduce a completely new system of global governance that will eliminate all today's global problems and take humanity to new heights.
Liaise with the current leadership pitching them on our new system and how this will benefit all mankind.
Form partnerships and links.
Write new laws and books laying the principles and rules to be adhered to.
Appointing bodies to implement the new global system.
Appoint members who form the Ultimate Executive Power; the Ultimate Judiciary Power and the Ultimate Legislative Power.
Appoint the new judiciary posts to implement and enforce the new system.
To appoint a project leader responsible for all global projects, designing, planning and building the Global Reserve Bank, etc.

4.2 Project implementation and development plan.

The Ultimate Executive Power to appoint a Project Leader who will assemble a team that will be responsible for the overall implementation of all projects, financial, fiscal, judiciary, governing, infrastructural, political, etc. in all countries.
These will see the successful implantation of the new system of governance, throughout the world.

4.3 The future structure of the Ultimate Executive Power.

When the implementation has taken place, the Ultimate Executive Power will comprise two Ultimate Executive Power

Presidents with equal powers meaning two equal [twin power] global Presidents. With the other Presidents acting as the equal yet opposing power suggesting alternatives but working together.

This will also consist of twenty-four national executive presidents representing their nations on a global scale. They will carry out the same duties together helping, the two Ultimate Executive Presidents to implement, enforce, monitor, alter and amend the constitution, the judiciary laws, the legislative laws, etc.

The founder the Ultimate Executive President shall select and nominate the second Ultimate President but if the twenty-four National Executive members have already taken their positions then they all shall vote in order to elect the second Ultimate President. If there is a tie, then the Ultimate Executive President shall cast the deciding vote. The member winning by the majority shall be appointed as the President.

When the number of leaders of Tomorrow's World Order representing us in all nations reaches forty-two the Ultimate Executive Power President can become seven having the highest office all working together. These seven can then choose who will be their leader too among them.

4.4 Role of the National Party Leader

The party leader shall represent the party's views and objectives national and globally.

Must contest elections with the aim to win and get into the highest political office of the country concerned.

Assess the feasibility of implementing our new system. Assess the obstacles and challenges and invent, develop and plan for solutions.

Has duties to see that the party will achieve its objectives of getting elected and winning the elections in order for the party to fulfill and realize its goals.

Advocate for the party's values to everyone.

Managing the party's business; proposing and developing

strategies to be considered and evaluated by the National Executive Power.

Involved in the implementation of the strategies approved by the National Executive Power.

To liaise with the Chairperson and the National Executive Power on challenging strategies formulating party policy.

Must be the communication piece pitching to potential supporters, members, donors, contributors and other people of interest who might help the party to achieve its goals.

Responsible for the managing of the members, making sure to some extent that the constitution complies with several other laws and regulations even though this is the duty of the compliance officer whom he can appoint.

Duties to implement the constitution and spearhead the party in the right direction.

Doing his or her best to make sure that the party will win the parliamentary elections.

Involved in policy development, communication, and implementation.

Vetoing and refusal of some laws and rules.

Responsible for the appointment of the Treasurer and the members of the National Executive Power.

Responsible for appointing a party chairperson and his or her deputy who if he or she is not around shall take over the proceedings of the meeting. If both are not available, the deputy shall assume the leadership roles for the sake of the meeting.

Shall act as the authorizing authority at the national level to give the final say when amendments to the constitution and bylaws are needed signing off documents, etc.

4.5 Election of the Party Leader

The Ultimate Executive Power can nominate party leaders for national posts initially and subsequently these can be elected and nominated through the voting system.

The party leader shall be elected to the role through voting by members whose subscriptions are up to date and are on the member's list. The candidate with the most votes shall become the leader and every member shall have a single vote. Potential candidate names are forwarded to the National Executive Power who will arrange the conference for voting inviting all eligible members to attend and cast a vote.

Elections can be called for when a party leader dies, resigns, or is voted out of office, etc. The National Executive Power shall call for an election within three months to replace that leader through voting. The National Executive Power must in the event of resignation or death hold elections within a month to replace the party leader.

They also have the power to elect an acting replacement within two weeks after the event until a new party leader is elected.

4.6 Term in office

The party leader shall have four years in office as a leader. Extensions can be agreed upon by the National Executive Power who shall decide for how long and normally for no more than two more years.

4.7 Role of the chairperson

He is employed by the Party Leader.

He can act as well as the Compliance officer who is there to make sure that the constitution of Tomorrow's World Order is in compliance with the requirements of the PPERA and the Equality Act and the Human Rights Acts etc. making sure everything does not conflict with these laws unless if a specific Compliance officer is already appointed.

In that case, he has to liaise with all including the Party Leader to make sure that everything is okay. If not okay; to arrange for rectifications informing the Party Leader or any appointed member within a specified time frame.

Takes the role of the leader when the leader is not available; needs initial approval though.

To encourage links and liaising of all members encouraging constructive-debate.

To ensure that all the Executive Power's policies are in the interest of the party.

To act as a checklist performer to make sure that the

recommendations of the National Executive Power are implemented by the Party Leader.

To sit in meetings noting the agenda and noting the important issues and making sure that these are discussed by the Executive Power.

To check and to maintain the highest standards and making sure that the constitution the bylaws etc. all comply, etc.

4.8 Use the following guideline to the creation of standardization, documentation, and procedural aspect to make it easy and mandate to comply with the relevant reporting and operational laws as in PPERA

4.8.1 Use Separation of Duties to,

Create and plan for a clear definition and plan that states who is responsible for what and when. Creating a workflow plan and a chart that is seen by all and distribute the information to all.

4.8.2 Use Access Controls,

Define who has access and to what. Define levels of access held by each committee member and who to see is one has limited access. There must be a flow chart showing the access chart with links and names of who has what kind of access and to what information and who is above that access hierarchy and when and how to get access if needed.

4.8.3 Use Physical Audits,

Tomorrow's World Order's financial committee must draw a plan that shows what information is held in physical form and what assets e.g. money in the petty cash safe is available and must be accounted and by who and when and how this is reported and to who?

4.8.4 The Financial Committee Must Standardize Documents;

Designing or ordering documents that will form the standard reporting system. A clear plan showing who is responsible for the documents in case some run out, who to complete what document and if they need verification of an authorizing signature who to do that and when and if not available who to take over.

4.8.5 Use Trial Balances.

A system must be in place to designate who and when can they rely on trial balance for reporting and compiling other documents. Periodic reconciliation is to be used to determine when and how and who will reconcile the books and balances and who to report to and if an authorization is needed to authorize the reports and sign them and who to do all that.

4.8.6 Use the Approval Authority.

The Financial Committee must appoint someone to act as the signing-off authority with duties to authorize the documents and processes.

The same person who will carry out the final audit or checks to make sure that all processes have been carried out according to the rules and procedures and that all this is in line with the Constitution and the rules and procedures of the country and as required by the PPERA. If that person is not around another option must be in place so that the deadline is met and that all documents meet the statutory requirements.

4.8.7 Establish and Define the Overseeing Body or Personnel.

The Financial Committee shall be the overseeing body to make sure there is compliance with the financial reporting laws. This is also responsible for monitoring the banking, insurance, real estate and in the managing of the securities of the party.
Deciding and informing the leader when to invest the party's funds which they don't need to use in the near future.

4.8.8 Delegation of Powers in Advance.

The leader of Tomorrow's World Order Party or the Treasurer can delegate some powers in advance usually at the beginning of taking office to the Financial Committee giving them operating powers in relation to the constitution. The Financial Committee will have powers to correct and take any action to correct any financial issues without the need to be authorized as authorization will have already been given at the beginning. They must see the overall financial aspect of the party budgeting, planning, monitoring, controlling and reporting all these.

4.8.9 Assign A Party Treasurer.

The party Treasurer shall be responsible for the Financial Committee and for reporting of financial statement purposes the Treasurer shall be the Approving authority, auditing and check listing documents before signing them and sending them to the Electoral Commission. The Treasurer must be appointed by the party leader and shall be in office for two to three years. He or she can resign, be voted off or dismissed by the leader. All resignation shall be in writing giving a two weeks' notice and handed to the Secretary or in his absence to any member of the National Executive Power who will forward the resignation to the Secretary or even President or party leader who will first negotiate to keep the person; if not to wish him or her farewell and arrange voting for a replacement and or appoint someone else within two weeks of resignation date, etc.

5   THE ULTIMATE EXECUTIVE POWER

This consist of;
The Ultimate Global Party Leader,
In the future- two Ultimate Global Party Leaders
A minimum group of seven country-specific Party Leaders that will rise to 24 leaders and then 42 leaders as more countries join in.
The Ultimate Secretary,
The Ultimate Treasurer,
The Head of the Global;
Financial Committees,
Standing Committee,
Project Development and Implementation,
The Head of the Global Reserve Bank,
The Head of FutureGoldCoin,
The Head of all Multi-national Companies,
The Head or Director of Tomorrow's World Order Party Foundation
The list is not exhaustive.

5.1 THE NATIONAL EXECUTIVE POWER

Shall consists of the;
The Nation-specific Party Leader,
The Treasurer,
The Secretary,
The Chairperson,
The Deputy Chairperson,
The Nominating Officer
The Campaigner,
Other non-office holding members. A minimum of seven is required.

If any person e.g. the leader holds one or more roles, some Party Officers of the party must be appointed and be present as members of the National Executive Power. The minimum number at any time must be seven even if the appointed ones have no specific titles.

All seven National Executive Power members have voting rights.

This is the National Executive Power that includes the Party leader who is the President as well.

Who will act as the Chairperson for the purposes of meetings who can delegate to his deputy or any party member?

There must also be a treasurer unless the leader is also the treasurer. The treasurer has an important role as the person responsible and required by the law to maintain an up to date of financial statements and transactions of the party.

The National Executive Power is made up of the Secretary who can also be the leader and the Treasurer as long as another person will be there in another role e.g. Nominating Officer or the Campaigner Officers.

5.2 Role of the National Executive Power

The powers of these members among them is to see that TWO [UK] is operating within the confines of the constitution and the rules of the country they are operating to make sure that the party can and will fulfill its objectives and aims as set out in the constitution.

They monitor all activities to make sure that the constitution is being followed and adhered to by all.

They are to put things in place, make amends, advance our vision to all and advocate our causes.

They hold and or delegate disciplinary meetings if no disciplinary committee exists.

They are involved in the day to day running of the party calling for extraordinary meetings when needed, holding campaigns and meetings with the aim of achieving party goals.

They can link with other organizations with the same interest for the purposes of carrying out their duties.

They can seek help from the global party on matters that are beyond their scope.

They represent the party in all United Kingdom and globally as to advance the values of the party.

The National Executive Power together with the party leader has powers to manage the members and everyone including those who are employed by the party and in the managing of the party's assets. They are responsible for setting up offices, purchasing offices, renting, leasing and the selling of purchased premises, etc. and with the help of the treasurer manage the party's funds efficiently and accurately.

The Executive Power has powers to approve parties' policies and manifestos in line with the constitutions.

The make the party leaders be answerable to them for accountability purposes.

The Secretary, who is a member of the National Executive Power has the main responsibility to maintain a register of all members ensuring that every member is registered according to the constitution.

Maintaining the register and checking payments as well and informing the treasurer on the financial aspects.

The Secretary in line with the constitution can link with the Chairperson in arranging meetings, etc.

He or she can take notes and minutes of the meeting and make sure that any relevant important communications are passed to the members.

Through the party leader, the National Executive Power can amend, write and correct the policies and rules of the Party at the local level and can consult the global leadership in complicated matters.

They have all the powers to hold meetings, disciplinary meetings, organize and hold annual general meetings, make sure that the constitution is followed, make sure that the laws of the country are being adhered to and in line with the constitution and take corrective action if not, managing the affairs of the party and represent Tomorrow's World Order in specific countries advancing our objectives.

6. OFFICE BEARERS OF THE PARTY

The party has a structure and a hierarchy with everyone with a specific role put down in a workflow plan with a chart showing who does what as required by specific laws with all these roles assigned to people and the structure written down so that anyone just need access to be party documents to know who to contact in case, they need help, etc. A clearly defined system with no ambiguity and in some cases with -on standby office bearers who will take over. Some posts to be appointed by the party leader and for some, the voting process is the method to be used. Office bearers can resign by handing written notice with a two weeks' notice period in which the leader must find a temporary replacement within two weeks. An election to be held four weeks after the resignation, death or removal of the candidate. If in conflict with the constitution or acting against it or disregard other laws against recommendations of the constitution, the office-bearer's role can be terminated in writing. The person has the right to be heard, to appeal and can choose to bring a friend or choose an offered-member of the party to represent him e.g. from another branch or country. Appeals can be made to the appeals board or committee and must be made within 28 days of the notice. The party leader can be appointed by the global leader or be elected through a voting system. He has four years in office which can be extended to a further year or two. Most office bearers' posts have either a two year or just a year term in which new members to be elected at the annual general meeting every year. According to law the Secretary is responsible for the day-to-day running of the party and all correspondence must be chosen or appointed for and all laws complied with so that the Electoral Commission can be notified.

6.1 The political party agent.

Requirements of the laws of some countries you must appoint and designate a post and office at Headquarters for the position of the party agent, but the party agent must also have another office separate from the Headquarters. This agent must be trusted with other party documents which he or she can keep away from the Headquarters.

The person appointed must make links and liaise with a lot of external people and departments like MPS, government agencies and even foreign MEPs.

He or she must be the link to the outside of the party and must report to the party leader who represents the party to the outside world.

Must have a detailed workflow plan written and all people he can liaise with be noted down. The person must act as well as a compliance officer ensuring that the party is complying with all electoral laws, etc.

He or she must represent the party where the party leader cannot and must complement the party leader's role rather than compete with.

He or she must have an office away from the headquarters and be given some documents as well he or she can keep at his or her office.

He or she can be neutral politically but must agree with our objectives and goals to a certain extent.

6.2 The treasurer

The national laws of some countries make it a must to have a treasurer who will report and submit all required legal documents and financial status of the party. You must appoint and designate a post and an office at Headquarters for the Treasurer. This will ensure compliance with the requirements of the electoral laws.

The Political Parties Electoral Referendum Act of 2000 places requirements on all political parties for the establishment of the Treasurer position. The law requires this Treasurer to keep an up-to-date record of all the activities and as such we have the Treasurer as [David Gomadza] and any changes will have to be reported to the Electoral Commission.

To make sure that the party complies with the requirements of the law and the Electoral Commission through the PPERA the Treasurer will head a small team to be employed by the party to be responsible for the finances of the party. A financial Committee must be appointed by the Party leader who is also the President.

7 THE DISCIPLINARY PROCESS

The code of conduct to be writing in the bylaws of all-party branches. The party leader, the Secretary and the National Executive Power to write down the bylaws using this constitution as the guiding principles. All complaints to be submitted in writing to the Secretary as appointed by the leader. Complaints to be heard in less than a week. The Disciplinary Committee to decide and in writing; to inform the person of his rights and rights of appeal if any. Stating the time limits and who and where to send the appeal. A clear process that must be followed.

7.1 The disciplinary committee.

Failure to comply with the requirements of the constitution, by-laws, and regulations will result in penalties or the need for a disciplinary meeting. The party leader must ensure that a party disciplinary committee exists to hear cases where members have disobeyed the rules.

Every member and employee on joining shall declare in writing when joining or signing employment documents that he or she will not;

Be involved in acts that conflict with the values and rules of the party.

That he or she will not be in competition with the party.

That the member should not join another political party whose views conflict with the part's views.

But when a breach occurs the issue must be sent to the disciplinary committee who will hear the case and pass judgment.

The member in breach must be informed that he can appeal and attend a meeting where he can bring a friend or be represented by appointed members of the party who will act in his or her best interest.

Time frames; 2 weeks to make an appeal and 28 days to appeal to the party leader or National Executive Power.

If still not resolved and issues are material, the party leader can forward this to the global leader for the final say.

Usually, the Party leader's decision is final.

8 RULES ON MEETINGS AND PROCEDURES.

The quorum is seven for the meeting to go ahead.

For the meeting to convene, there must be at least three-party officials or more if the other party officer holds one or more positions e.g. the leader who also happens to be the treasurer. In most cases, there must be a party leader and or the appointed Chairperson or deputy specifically appointed for meetings, the Treasurer and the Secretary at any given meeting.

Meetings to be held once every month unless if it is a campaigning period which can determine the frequency. These should be on the last weekend of the month.

The Annual General Meeting to be held once every year after August and before 1 December where the progress is discussed for that year. Notice of four weeks to be given to all members, especially those with voting rights.

Motions to be discussed at the meeting to be handed to the person responsible especially the Chairperson or Secretary two weeks before the date of the meeting.

Where there is voting; to appoint new members to different positions for the new year.

Time to set new agendas and challenges.

A chance for the party leader to pitch the members and ask for questions, suggestions, etc.

Time for the Treasurer to give an update on the financial situation of the party.

A time to provide and collect information to be used for the compilation of the financial statements of the party.

Voting can be by raising the hands or electronically and where there is a tie the party leader or chairperson can make the final vote the decider.

The meeting shall be recorded as minutes. These minutes must state the date, time and venue of the meeting including the start time of the meeting.

The minutes must indicate those who were present at the meeting stating the full name and the role of the person.

It must state who was absent and why.

The minutes must record in note point the matters arising from the meeting and what happened, and issues raised.
The minutes must also include the next date and time of the meeting as agreed in the meeting.

9 DETAILS REGARDING THE KEEPING UP OF THE PARTY'S ACCOUNTS

*Detailed listings of all the roles, identifying and allocating tasks to the people and putting in place a process that makes it mandatory to comply with the law requirements. There must be a system in place that is checked and followed and proven that it makes the party comply with all the requirements. A compliance officer role to oversee this must be appointed and or the party leader to take the leading role to make sure this is so. There must be the testing of the procedures, way before the deadline. Document and standardization to be adopted with the party leader or chairperson or secretary be chosen as the authorizing authority signing off documents after the check listing and auditing to all in line with the constitution and the requirements of other laws like the PPERA. The paperwork and documentation must be kept, and copies kept at a different location in electronic form advisably given to the party's agent to keep. A clear workflow plan to be drawn to show who specifically is responsible for the finance, the running of day-to-day, dealing with all queries, external forces, and other organizations with the same objectives and values as those of our party. The name of the authorizing authority who signs off everything must be written down on the workflow chart and there must be easy access to this information. Make sure you appoint a **Party Agent**. This person can be politically neutral usually external who has the mandate to lodge disclosure with the relevant body. This person must keep records of the part also at their office which is not the same as the party's headquarters.*

9.1 Rules for forming tomorrow's world order's committees

The following guidelines and bylaws must be used to form any party committees.
The Ultimate Executive Power and or the Ultimate Party leader to form all global committees e.g. the Financial Committee, the Judiciary Committee, The Enforcing Committee, The Standing Committee, etc. At the national level the National Executive

Power and or the National Party Leader to appoint the committee leader who will appoint and allocate tasks, etc.

All committees where the country-specific laws stipulate that registration is required and must be registered; to do so and the link to the party be declared that the committee will be responsible for the day-to-day running of Tomorrow's World Order.

The committee must field a candidate to enter the contest with the hope to represent the party at the national committee level.

Appointed committee leader to put a committee hierarchy and task structure clearly defining who is who and what they do in the committee.

Must have all process that ensures day-to-day operations and compliance is met.

A compliance officer can be appointed to check compliance with the constitution and all country-specific laws.

All committees to be guided and must abide by the party's laws, constitution and bylaws and must acknowledge that they exist only to fulfill the tasks of Tomorrow's World Order.

They must not compete, frustrate or bring into disreputation the values of Tomorrow's World Order.

Must acknowledge that they are quasi-subsidiaries of Tomorrow's World Order.

Committees must be involved in ongoing activities e.g. promoting the party through campaigns and fundraising.

Must publish and advertise party materials printing leaflets and newsletters etc. and remain active.

All national committees to have their own headquarters that can be or separate from party headquarters, etc.

Must hold the Committee convention for the party's work, etc.

The National Executive Power of each country to create bylaws to govern the functions of all committees in line with the constitution or country rules.

Where permanent committees don't exist, there can be temporary committees during presidential or prime-ministerial election years that can help with the campaigning and all day-to-day operations of the campaigning year.

9.2 Names of committees and the duties of each committee.

Every committee must have a chair, a secretary, treasurer, press officer, and a membership secretary.

All national committees to hold annual general meetings where new committee members can be selected, appointed, or voted to their respective tasks.

Committee to abide by all files and reports reporting requirements within the constitution, bylaws and national rules, etc.

New committee members to be elected or appointed every year at the annual general meeting or the national conference.

To be nominated on merit by the committee leaders and some might be politically neutral in that they are needed because of their qualifications rather than affiliation to our political party but better if they don't belong to a party that has views, we are against.

9.3 Establish the financial committee

9.3.1 Financial Committee

The Party Leader/ the President has powers to appoint a Financial Committee and has a mandate to do so in order for the party to comply with the requirements of the PPERA and other political parties' laws. The Party Leader must appoint, name and record the members of the team and what their objectives are and what is required of them. There must be a plan showing who is who as members. What duties each is responsible to do. When and how often they are to do what they are supposed to do. The Financial Committee must formulate, devise, implement, monitor and plan the internal financial controls to be used and be adopted by the committee and party in order to meet the requirements of the PPERA. The financial Committee must create systems that will make sure that the party adheres to the requirements of PPERA. The committee must observe and use the following procedures;

9.3.2 Finance.

All donations, contributions, raised money, loans, etc. are to be used in accordance with the constitution and for the realization of the party's objectives. Any payments must be done by the Treasurer and depending on the amount involved might require the signature of the party leader or Secretary. Procedures must be in place to comply with the compliance rules which means all accounts to be audited and assessed once a year before the Treasurer sends them to the Electoral Commission. Expenses can be paid to the Executive Powers for expenses incurred during performing their duties.

10 GLOBAL RESERVE BANK.

This will act as the world reserve bank accepting deposits of all new fresh printed money of each and every country.

Managing funds and reserves keeping an up-to-date account of all transactions.

Managing our own currency, the FutureGoldCoin making sure that the digital currency is run and well managed to check its security and suitability of use both as a world currency for all transactions and as a reserve currency.

Involved in the issuing of our Futuregoldcoin to all nations in proportion to the deposited funds.

Assessing the circulating levels making sure that every country has enough of our money.

Maintaining savings accounts of all nations calculating interest earned.

The global reserve bank leader who is appointed by the Ultimate Executive Power to manage the deposited funds and investing some to generate more.

To set aside a percentage of the reserves towards global development projects liaising with the Project Development Team.

The reserve development fund will allocate funds for projects to be completed in weeks or months by ensuring that money for the whole project is available even before the projects start.

The idea is to carry out huge projects before even paid a cent of the money.

We shall use the deposits as collateral and as long as the nation is sovereign, we shall use this as the easy ability to print money and their word as a guarantee that we will get the money back. This speed up the building and completion of projects even without receiving any money.

To make sure that all nations to deposit a base value of the deposits; that is the minimum reserve that forms the minimum balance.

To report to the National Executive Powers and maybe twice a year all to meet to discuss progress and plan for the future.

Twice as a minimum a year to link with the Ultimate Executive Power to update on progress and plan for the future.

To make sure that all nations are using two currencies; their sovereign currency and our digital currency by auditing countries reporting those who are not to the enforcement power to be appointed initially by the Ultimate Executive Power or Ultimate Global Leader.

To form multi-national companies.

To arrange the funding in advance of all that is needed.

To offer loans to multinationals to carry out swift projects.

To assess the savings of all nations and using this as collateral to provide infrastructure and services needed by that country and start the building projects even without payment as long as approved by the Ultimate Executive Power and or the Global Party Leader.

To determine the time frames for the global printing of new money.

To put corrective fiscal measures to flatten out any obstacles, etc.

To report to the Ultimate Executive Power and the Global President or Party Leader.

11 TOMORROW'S WORLD ORDER PARTY FOUNDATION.

To be created by the Ultimate Executive Power and or by the Global Party Leader the main reason for its establishment is to

source funds for investment through donations and sponsorship and to act as a perpetual fund that will fund our party through the proceeds of the investment so that every nation can receive a grant donated from this fund to help establish TWO party all over the globe providing easily funds for political agendas.
The directors and investors will not be interested in the profits so there are no dividends to be paid.
The donors must be informed that their money to help our political cause.
The foundation is a not-for-profit in that the donated money is kept by the foundation and no directors to be paid dividends.
The foundation exists to fund Tomorrow's World Order political party.

11.1 Fundraising and money donated to the Foundation

The donated money is fenced in that it is not used but is kept for a long time being used for investment only the profits made can be transferred to Tomorrow's World Order's account money that can be used for paying employees, for consumables and services, etc.
The donated money to be invested and the proceeds only to be channeled to Tomorrow's World Order account.
One to be developed in each country and a dedicated team be established to source funds from potential donors.
A huge recruitment drive of fundraisers to fund that foundation.

12 FUTUREGOLDCOIN DEVELOPMENT EXECUTIVE

The Ultimate Executive Power and or the Global Party Leader will appoint the FutureGoldCoin Development Executive to design its own digital currency, develop, implement, monitor, check and audit for security and feasibility, etc. continuously.
This executive to be involved in the implementation of our digital currency global and its maintenance.

To establish Executive branches globally.
To recruit a team of experts who see the implementation and monitoring in every country solving issues that might arise.
Monthly official meetings and quarterly of all global teams and at least two annual conferences together with the Ultimate Executive Power.

13 UNIVERSAL ENFORCING AND JUDICIARY EXECUTIVE POWER.

The Ultimate Executive Power and or the Global Party Leader to establish the Universal Enforcing and Judiciary Executive Power which has a duty to enforce our laws globally. This executive power will further establish executive powers in every county that will enforce our laws.

Our laws are universal, and crime is punishable in any other country irrespective of where it was committed.

To appoint and train a special enforcement unit that is directly answerable to the Ultimate Executive Power and or the Global Leader showing their powers to remove anyone's individual immunity.

Must bring people to justice no matter where the crimes were committed.

The Ultimate Executive Power and or the Global Party Leader appoint the new judiciary system to deal with violators.

These to enforce our laws and rules globally safeguarding our interests and everyone's interests globally.

14 MECHANISMS FOR CHANGING THE CONSTITUTION

This constitution is the guiding line of changing and amending the constitution. The party's decision-making board can give notice in writing to all voters and members with rights giving notice of two to four weeks. Must arrange the venue and time and be involved in the voting and as a general rule two-thirds is enough to amend the constitution. Material changes must be referred to as the global Ultimate Executive Power and the Global Party Leader who will authorize the go-ahead of the amendments. The quorum at such meetings must be greater or equal to seven with each member having a single vote apart from the party leader who can cast another vote in case of a tie.

14.1 Rules on amendments to the constitution.

Intentions to amend the constitution should be announced to everyone four weeks before the Annual General Meeting or a special Extraordinary General Meeting is held at any time as long as the members are notified of the intention two weeks before the date of the EGM. This is normally for minor amendments but if the changes are substantial, the global branch must be notified, and all proposals are forwarded to this global branch who will look at the proposed changes in order to check if the changes are material to require the signature of the authorizing authority.

After authorization the TWO [UK] branch can now announce the intention to make amendments two weeks before the day of the meeting. Everyone with voting rights must attend and vote. Two-thirds of the votes are enough for the constitution to be amended. Any changes to be forwarded to the global branch to be synchronized if needed globally.

15 ESTABLISHMENT OF STATE AND TERRITORY BRANCHES

Apart from this constitution also follow local country-specific laws in branch and territory establishment of branches and also the party leaders to check with the global leader to make sure that the national goals are in line with the global goals.

The party leader together with the National Executive Power can establish or nominate someone to be responsible for the expansion.

To check and create bylaws as seen fit.

Representation can be addressed by local bylaws and the party leader together with the National Executive Power to oversee or delegate such tasks.

To draw up a detailed expansion plan showing dates and time frames needed to establish a branch in other territory and to complement the national and global plan.

To set up a team with a project manager or leader to arrange the funding and liaise with the national party leader to appoint roles to fill these new branches.

16 ENDORSING CANDIDATES

The Party Leaders together with the National Executive Power to put a detailed plan of endorsing candidates who stand in all elections as this is the main objective of the party. The candidates must understand and have the aim to contest, win and take office so that our party can realize and implement their goals.

The party Secretary or Chairperson or any office role deemed to be so on request by the Party Leader must organize a public meeting or gathering like a conference four weeks before the date and announce inviting people to attend.

Endorse only candidates that have signed and agreed to comply with our constitution and standards for credibility purposes.

Must work together with the Campaigning Committee to rally support and ensure full capacity or a large gathering.

Distribution of campaigning materials well ahead of the date to ensure a large turn-out.

The Party Leader to endorse the candidate to run for elections.

Meetings to be held during the week at night after work or weekends where the party leader must travel to the constituent.

At the conference the candidate to take the stage together with the Party Leader who endorses him or her publicly and live on party broadcast. Heralding to the world that he or she is the candidate to represent Tomorrow's World Order in the upcoming election.

The Party Leader publicly endorse the candidate giving him 100% support before rallying everyone to back the candidate.

Leaflets and other publications to be distributed before and after the endorsement with the picture of the candidate visible for all to see.

All endorsement must be viewed and regarded as Official Endorsement with a procedure in place to write and record down this in party books and documents showing the date, time, venue and who endorsed the person and a picture of the party leader with the candidate taken and put in a file.

Only party leaders have powers to endorse and in case of absences the conference can be postponed or a party leader from another country be invited to perform the ceremony.

Anyone from the Ultimate global Executive Power has the right to endorse and can do so as authorized by the Global Party Leader.

Ideally, the endorsement to be broadcast on national television and the Secretary or Treasurer to arrange that or delegate such activities.

17 COMMENCEMENT

The party leaders and the National Executive Power Board to choose a date, a venue and send out notices giving a four weeks' notice to all who can vote to invite them to attend and vote so that the constitution is commenced, and this noted as the day the constitution takes effect. All participants to vote to adopt the constitution signing to confirm that. The party leader and the National Executive Power to sign the adoption motion.

A date is to be set aside where and announced to all informing the willingness to vote in order to commence the constitution on that specific date.

Notice to be sent four weeks given as notice to all those with voting rights and two weeks' notice to members to attend.

The National Executive and the Party leader and every member must be present to cast a vote in favor of commencement.

Everyone on the day to vote to adopt the constitution on that specific date and time.

The National Executive Power and the Party Leader to sign the motion of commencing the constitution.

All this to be publicized in the Official Magazine of the party and most local newspapers.

An Official Magazine to be printed and distributed free showing the day the constitution commenced.

This date to be noted and written down in all official documents and be regarded as the commencement date of the constitution and thereafter everyone to be abided by it.

18 DISSOLUTION

Dissolving the party in a specific area or branch requires first the approval of the Global Party Leader and or that of the Ultimate Executive Power. A letter of intent must be sent to the Global Headquarters four weeks before the intended meeting to vote to dissolve the branch or party. Members and or assets can be passed onto another branch or party where necessary. After the voting to dissolve the Party Leader or representative of the branch must inform the Global Leader no later than two weeks after the meeting to seek the authorizing signature to dissolve that branch or party. The Global Leader's decision is final.

Any winding up of the party is to be authorized by the Global Party Leader or the Ultimate Executive Power in case of his or her absence who has the final word and no subsidiary party groups can wound up the party until after authorization in which a meeting must take place and the members with voting rights vote. Two-thirds of the votes are enough for the dissolution to take place.

19 INTERPRETATION

In this constitution the following words are defined here;

TWO means Tomorrow's World Order

AGM means Annual General Meeting

NEP means National Executive Power
NEPB means National Executive Power Board
PPERA means
UEP means Ultimate Executive Power

PART 3

TOMORROW'S WORLD ORDER'S SOVSUPERIUSCOGENS

1. WHAT ARE THE SOVSUPERIUSCOGENS?

These are Tomorrow's World Order guiding principles, rules and compelling laws that establish who we are, what we stand for, what we do and how we impact and influence the world around us and to a large extent these define how we expect all nations under the sun to operate and respond. Further, these set the rules, principles, standards, and norms that govern all global nations. Clearly setting the rules and what is expected of them. These Sovsuperriuscogens are based on the following principles;

1.1. Sovereignty:

Firstly:

In relation to Tomorrow's World Order, this signifies that we are not related to any nation, nor do we belong to any nation, nor that we represent any nation. We are sovereign in our right and we are not subject to any control by any nation and having said that we are fair and represent the whole world as a whole rather than the interests of individual nations.

Secondly:

We strongly believe in the individual state sovereignty as the fundamental principle and pivotal aspect of any nation. The main idea behind our core principles is the idea of individual state sovereignty as a prerequisite to any progress and development. We believe for any nation to progress successfully

it must be a sovereign nation with all key attributes associated with sovereignty. Without an individual's state's sovereignty then there can never be the talk of progress and development.
Thirdly:
The idea of individual nation's sovereignty goes beyond realizing that individuals have powers to mind their own affairs without any intrusion, guidance, etc. as in this case any uninvited interferences are regarded as acts of aggression in which a nation is entitled under our laws to self-defend itself using any force necessary. The emphasis and difference to the current system is the fact that all nations are capable and expected to be responsible for their own development and growth. There can never be interference unless if that specific nation has formally requested that. There is no nation or entity that can declare to act on another nation's interest. It is one nation for itself and only Tomorrow's World Order for us all. This, as you will see later on, will draw a line between manipulation, abuse for own gains and devious acts where nations pretend to help others but actually enslaving indirectly or stalling development as to maintain a situation of dependence something that is against sovereignty.
If a nation is a sovereign one, there is no talk of aid, helping, leading another, etc. simply because that nation is sovereign and as such can and is expected to be responsible for its own affairs without any outside interference. Such interferences are regarded as express acts of aggression unless expressly requested by the nation to do so.
Fourthly:
The main theme of our values hangs upon the fact that we believe that;
The government is forever indebted to its people and therefore is there to serve the people not the other way round. This indebtedness to its people comes from the printing of new money process. We strongly believe that every government when it prints new money, it owes its citizens this money. For accounting purposes, every transaction must have a debit and a credit value in the trial balance. Therefore, when the

government prints money it technically or metaphorically writes the 'I owe you' to the people. Printing money increases the value of the people. So, our new system acknowledges this so that in the future the government must 'pay back this money and settle the 'I owe you' I mentioned above. This places the burden on the government to bail-out people through loans, mortgages, etc. when they default and are at risk of losing their wealth and savings. Since printing money is forever, this means the government is indented to its citizens forever. That places the burden to look after its own people bailing-them out, unlike the current system that bails-out banks. The same banks stealing through Payment Protection Insurance from the citizens the little money they have [-a pre-planned embezzling trick nevertheless in small amounts so as to avoid being caught].

1.2. The ever indebtedness vicious cycle and the burden to act swiftly placed on the government's part.

Printing money; means the government generating money from nowhere and as a responsible government must owe this money to the citizens. Injection of this money into the economy increases wealth, production and demand. It increases the disposable income that in turn increases growth and production. Soon everything will increase for a time until when the money in circulation and that with the people starts to decrease yet consumption remains high. Soon the people are left without enough cash for the increased consumption. They start defaulting on loans and mortgages. They start using their savings until a time they start even selling their property before going burst. The system collapses before the governments realize what is going on and jump in when all wealth is destroyed, and things are irrecoverable.

Our system places the 'burden to act' on the government. The time it prints money it owes its citizens the value of this money. That places the duty of care and to protect them on the government and mandates to them responsibilities to act swiftly and proactively. The government because of this relationship must;

Act swiftly and plan ahead to pay back the 'I owe you' generated from the printing of new money.

They must act to protect and preserve the wealth of the people.

Must act fast to bail-out the people and not banks.

Must do everything to protect the savings and the wealth of the people.

Must provide loans, mortgages to the people before a financial crisis arises.

Must print new money and through our new system of a government-held savings account must assess eligibility and offer cheaper low-cost loans, mortgages, pay for health, pension, etc.

This is the only way the government pays back the 'I owe you' created by the printing of money.

Our system means the wealth preserved and the government running to the rescue before wealth is destroyed.

The process, if repeated continuously with loans, help, and mortgages, etc. given to the people from printed money through the government-owned savings account where the money can then be transferred to the person's own savings or current account will see increases in wealth.

This guarantees the extraordinary never seen before building up of wealth to levels we can only dream of.

1.3. Absolute power:

We believe that we are and must be the world's ultimate or

absolute power in that only we have the power to have the final say, the power to lead and guide all nations, the power to direct the course of action and to spearhead development. This status is an acquired status based on our suitability and credibility to represent every one's interest without bias as we don't belong to any military, religious or political cult, nor do we represent a minority-special-privileged elite, etc. We stand for everyone and as such we are the only fair unbiased power to act responsibly as a global leader. We have our own system that is effective and fit-for-purpose in that it relates to the current and future environment be it, political, social, religious, economic, financial, etc. or otherwise. This also means that we have an enforcement system to see that our rules and laws are observed by all equally without giving unnecessary special privileges to certain individuals as the current system does. The system in which we are saying that it is outdated and obsolete as evidenced by the fact that they don't follow their own rules and as such we can't expect them to act fairly. We have to act as the law upholders and overseers. Our absolute power is based on the fact that a school needs a headmaster, so as a college needs a principle, just like a country needs a prime minister, president or chancellor the globe needs a global leader hence the rise of Tomorrow's World Order.

I empathize here that organizations like the UN, NATO, etc. can't and will not be regarded as global leaders as they are biased, created by the individual's states of the founding nations, and represent an elite special group, etc. whose interest they represent, and the talk of absolute power is nonexistence. An absolute power in this sense is one that can guide all unbiased and be fair to represent everyone and act on behalf of all mankind.

1.4. Empowering everyone.

The current system is based on dependence just like all evil systems in the past e.g. slavery. The fact that the current system functions well when the individual nation's sovereignty is trampled on is a gross miscarriage of justice and proves that the current system is not fit for the purpose. The current system as

I advocated in my book: Tomorrow's World Order is based on one big parasite feeding on everyone else's pains and misery and or depending on others for growth and development at the expense of everyone else. This can only mean the removal of an individual state's sovereign and once that happens then a situation of dependence, threats, intimidation, dirty tricks and manipulation becomes the norm. This is the only way this nation can grow at the expense of everyone else. We strongly, vehemently and profusely are against this. We stand for the empowering of every nation on earth.

1.5. Raising global standards and wealth of all nations.

We have plans and solutions to make every nation on earth experience growth to levels never achieved before.
Experience wealth levels to never thought of as possible before.
We are to raise living standards globally to levels never dreamt of in our lifetime. We believe the only way is through acknowledging and emancipating every nation on earth first through making all sovereign in their own right.
Removing all things that take away the nation's sovereign. The only way to increase global development to levels never seen before is through recognizing and accrediting all nations as sovereign.
We are going to impose minimum standards globally and any nations below these standards are answerable to us.

1.6. Providing peace to all mankind.

We have a mandate to provide global peace through our laws and rules. We have laws and regulations to ban wars, weapons, killings of women and children, providing a peaceful environment through the banning of fossil fuels in favor of clean renewable energy sources, etc.
Peace for all must mean just that.
Our laws will close all loopholes in the current systems and put

tough laws to bring perpetrators to justice.

We have the E-laws to help us deal with evil where women and children die needlessly simply because no-one feels empathy towards these as they don't relate to them. This is not based on discrimination, no but by the fact that it is human nature to regard or ignore those we are not familiar with, etc.

1.7. Effective Justice system

Our legal system is based on peremptory international compelling laws that have international jurisdiction. This means any crime can be tried in any country on earth and by anyone as long as they are sworn apparatus to deal with the law and legal system.

This is different from the current system where evil gets away as they are given immunity in other nations or zones, etc.

Our system has international jurisdictions even in own country in that one will be brought to justice no matter what as long as that person is alive.

Our system will remove all time periods as this is abused as nations commit serious crimes in the hope of putting new laws after they have carried evil acts and got what they wanted giving them immunity but the same nations become strict to the offenders after that law has been passed. Making the offender keep offending citing the evil acts of the people purporting to punish such crimes. It's like pointing to a log in one's eye when you have even a bigger log in your own eye. That is not good for justice.

1.8. Making the law a source of peace and comfort for those who seek justice.

We must and are obliged to provide an effective legal system that is observed by all and adhered to by all and feared by all but above all respected by all. We must provide a source of hope and comfort for all. This is only achievable through an effective system. This can act as a deterrent as well.

1.9. Providing an effective system to solve all current global problems namely:

Poverty,
Human rights abuses,
Torture,
Human-hacking-slavery,
Wastage and global, national and individual debt,
Poor infrastructure,
Poor living standards,
Pollution and poor-quality air,
Global warming,
Dependence on defense and wastages in terms of missed opportunities,
Corruption,
Secret slavery,
Unfair manipulative practices in some countries where they use bio-digital and cyber weapons and or other agents to gain a competitive advantage, robbing people using these agents, controlling people using these agents,
Chipping of people with devices that emits radiation,
Man-made viruses, bio-agents, cyber weapons, digital weapons,
Genocide,
Secret making of advanced but already-outlawed weapons e.g. making digital viruses that act and mimics the outlawed biological ones with the same effect,
Crimes against humanity,
Crimes of aggression,
Useless institutions perpetuating the problems,
Squashing of other nations' sovereignty through unnecessary loans, extreme use of force e.g. through use of nukes to spread fear and submission,
Killing of own people in favor of national security as in false flagging,
Government encouraging and sponsoring terrorist activities by hacking their own people leaving them with little option, torturing them to commits acts of violence against others in retaliation or as a way out of torture,

Violations of international laws over national security,
Engaged in acts of aggression and sabotage to justify military
action etc.,
Misuse and mismanagement of financial resources e.g.
channeling funds to make weapons at the expense of living
standards etc.,
Lack of guts, especially for those in power as a crime under the
E-laws governments must do whatever for their people,
Grouping into a cult that acts to intimidate others directly or
indirectly the idea here is that if a company can be forced to
break into smaller ones, why can't a global threat to peace be
forced to do so? If a gang is meant to be squashed why can't a
cult that does the same evil?
Including many others.

1.10. To provide a clear framework and guiding principles to be adhered to and followed by all those this might relate to.

A clear justice framework that is not ambiguous and is
understood and respected by all is the only answer. The legal
system must be considered as fair to function well.

1.11. Provide stability to all systems.

A global leader's presence and sound enforcement and judiciary
system is a source of trust, peace, and stability to all. That
removes the fear and intimidation climate posed by the presence
of gangs, cults or evil superpowers. This is the only source of
true global peace and stability.

2 SCOPE AND PURPOSE OF TOMORROW'S WORLD ORDER.

2.1. Reasons behind the rise of Tomorrow's World Order.

A lack of an effective system that is not only fit for purpose but also up to date and representing all mankind.

A system that is adhered to by all and is respected and feared by all as well.

The current system has crashed or crashed years ago witnessed by;

continuous wars, financial crisis 2008 being the final straw, gross moral decadence,

poor living standards even now for the developed countries,

poor human rights records globally, global warming and climatic change, outbreaks of diseases, development, and possession of weapons of mass destruction [WMDs], lack of networking and cooperation,

poor infrastructure globally still to 1980s levels; all these points to a system not fit for purpose.

Outdated systems that are now obsolete.

In relation to the above point is the fact that the current system is out of date because it is no longer observed or adhered to even by the owners of the system in that now they ignore and or do not follow their own rules choosing to ignore their own courts, judiciary forms, and other subsidiary systems.

Stuck in defensive systems of development.

Inferior thinking and lack of foresight have meant that humanity remains in the defensive systems where the main rationale is that of making cheaper weapons and use the weapons to get all the expensive resources like oil through wars, sanctions, invasions, and attacks killing thousands of women and children in the process. Something we strongly are against.

Lack of a global leader who is unbiased and represent the wishes of all mankind.

A leader to lead the way and take humanity out of the defensive systems, restoring peace and providing wealth to levels never witnessed before.

Stalling of development and a lack of global wealth improvement.
The levels of development have not changed since the 1980s the developed nations are still developed, and the developing are still developing even now with some developed nations showing the same signs as those of developing countries showing not just stagnating global wealth but declining living standards as well.

A lack of foresight and knowledge to understanding global systems and what is needed to solve global problems.
We have global debt above $244 trillion, we have poverty globally, financial crisis, poor wealth levels, above all there is no effective platform to tackle global problems. One that provides a way to deal with all these issues.

A lack of a universal justice system that is unbiased and represent all mankind.
A system that makes sure that the global laws are observed if not then punish the violators. A system that provides a clear framework of rules, regulations, and laws that safeguards humanity and ensures the continuation of humanity. A system and legal framework to guide, monitor and control all nations under the sun. A system not attached to any country and one that does not represent any country but a system that is fair and acts as the global leader. The rationale behind this being that a school has a headmaster, a university counselor, a country a leader in a Prime Minister, President or Councilor, but the globe has no leader. This is the root of all problems hence the rise of Tomorrow's World Order. Even though some nations had tried to juggle and take the role of a global leader, but national interest has often conflicted with the role of a global leader and in some cases with serious consequences taking the 9/11 for example. I have explained why the elected institutions like the UN etc. can never be global leaders. Read; Tomorrow's World Order.

The lack of a monitoring system.
A system to monitors all countries and several institutions globally laying down laws, rules, and regulations all with the aim to provide a smooth and effective system that eradicates and eliminates all global problems.

3 TOMORROW'S WORLD ORDER'S AIMS, GOALS, AND OBJECTIVES.

3.1 Overall global goals.

a. Spearhead global growth and wealth to levels never experienced before.

To take developed nations to very advanced nations and to take all developing countries to the very developed nations and further with time. Our system will increase every nation's and individual wealth to levels never seen before. We aim to achieve all this by adopting and advancing growth policies and laws. That means banning austerity measures globally. We shall provide a system that increases growth in all areas exponentially.

We shall remove everything that hinders, stampedes on or stifle growth. We aim to boost the economies of all nations under the sun. Living standards must and shall increase as we shall put laws defining what is expected and enforce these laws. We have rules that will help every nation and those in power to choose policies that will increase growth and wealth exponential.

b. Provide a financial system that focuses on global, national and individual wealth.

Our system removes the current system by proposing the only way to increase growth by increasing the printing of money the only thing that increases growth and wealth. We have a method that works.

A method that takes hyperinflation into account and providing the only way to increase wealth exponentially taking every nation to levels never seen before. We have a holistic approach that will see all this take place. Our system works [see our financial plan] and will spearhead the growth of national and global wealth to new heights. This system will have five or more continuous money printing cycles to boost growth and wealth.

The current system is self-contradictory and the way it is designed means for decades there can never be growth. What only happens is that period of growth is inevitably followed by a period of decline. This is because of the system. The current system emphasizes austerity measures; living within your means. People save and don't spend much until the levels where the economy struggles only for that government to be ousted out of power. The other party then only works to restore the growth and wealth lost until they are taken out of power because there is a limit, they can do because of the influx of fresh new money is limited. What is happening for eight years on average [the period of a party they can be in power] are periods of growth followed by decline. Our system eliminates this and replaces austerity by a growth drive for say 5 years then another cycle after that with one or two years in between where the money is not printed but the emphasis here is own trading. We will have our own digital currency as well as the fiat that will help all nations tackle hyperinflation and increase wealth to new levels. See our money plan. In short, we will have our currency the FutureGoldCoin that will act as the New Single Reserve Global Currency [NSRGC]. The advantage is that we are not tied to any country. Any nation will benefit greatly by using our currency as the NSRGC. This is the only way to increase national wealth to new levels and increase growth and development. We as global leaders will set laws and targets for wealth and growth patterns. Every nation will implement our 5-year growth plan that is a blanket-plan globally. As each nation is sovereign, they will have the right to print new money. For five years all nations on earth will print money as the only true source of new money. To fight hyperinflation and other problems with printing money we as the global leaders have a Global Reserve Bank [GRB]. This is a bank where nations will have to deposit the newly printed money in exchange for our universal currency the FutureGoldCoin. So, every nation will print their own new money and then hands this money to us which we deposit for them in our GRB as their deposits or savings. We then give them the equivalent of their money in our currency the FutureGoldCoin which is digital. They then take this FutureGoldCoin in digital form or fiat depending on the stage we are in of development and use in their economy. This is to stop over flooding their economy thereby lowering the value of the economy and their currency. Instead, their money remains valuable and at the same time, they will have savings with our bank that earns interest as well. First, this empowers all nations and eliminates the need to borrow from say the IMF. Secondly, this eliminates any global debt in the future. We have a plan for dealing with national and global debt too. Every nation will then be able to lower their own currency's value against our FutureGoldCoin to increase exports of their goods. This lowering of currency value makes their exports attractive boosting exports and increasing their forex base. This has the advantage that their economy can increase the production of goods to the highest levels to meet the new money in the economy. This fights hyperinflation steering growth. The second advantage is that since we are independent of any country our NSRGC will not devalue their own currency.

The current problems of using the USA's currency as the Single Reserve Global Currency are that;

First;

All countries automatically lose their sovereignty the moment they use this currency as a reserve currency. This is because they automatically follow whatever the federal authorities set as their monetary policies. This automatically makes every nation exists only to serve the USA's interests in that in the end only the USA will see meaningful growth. All nations will automatically become under the USA and the USA alone can increase production and sell to all other countries who use their currency. All other nations act as markets for the USA to dump all the extra goods created by the new money. This makes only the USA print new money viably as a means of growth and if others try the same, they suffer economic decline.

Secondly;

All the other countries are left with no alternative but to rely on loans and handouts from the USA. The USA can determine who it gives loans and handouts through say the World Bank and the IMF and making it control the flow of money to its advantage and through sanctions as a monetary weapon. Punishing some nations and putting demands that steer their growth and demand so they keep growing where no other nation will see any meaningful growth. This enables the USA to gather all the resources it wants cheaply simply by controlling the flow of their money through sanctions etc. Creating a hungry situation when it gets what it wants e.g. oil then remove the sanctions and might even donate newly printed money in $millions or $billions [which is valueless to them as they can simply print this in a flash] to the country that was on sanctions to increase demand of their goods stimulating demand for their goods or of their subsidiary partners.

Thirdly;

The use of the USA currency globally by all nations as the reserve global currency disadvantages the USA itself. This is because the USA, in this case, has no other separate currency it can use as a reserve currency. Its normal currency is the same as the reserve currency. In other words, they don't have a reserve currency they can manipulate to increase exports and development. They can't lower the currency as what other nations can do. The USA has strongly condemned China accusing it of manipulating its currency playing dirty taking advantage of the USA, etc. This is untrue and even if it's true, this is not intentional. To China, this is a survival strategy. What you must understand is that for China this is a tactic to fight hyperinflation and steer growth increasing exports to meet the new money. The USA sees this tactic as a cheating part of China because the USA no matter what; will always feel cheated by all nations because they don't have a separate reserve currency to do the same. So, our system will benefit the USA the most as they can do the same as what China is doing if they use our FutureGoldCoin as the Reserve Currency as we are not linked to any country.

c. Increasing wealth exponentially eliminating debt in the process.

Firstly;

Our financial system eliminates the above issues by empowering every nation to be sovereign and never lose that sovereignty. Sovereignty means the right to print own money and right to determine the course of each nation's development. That means avoiding costly IMF or World Bank loans which emphasizes austerity measures hence the stifled growth over the past seventy years. Every nation can print its own currency and deposit this in our Global Reserve Bank. That creates deposits or savings. They use our FutureGoldCoin in their economy as the base money using it to set prices in digital form to fight hyperinflation. Using local currency during the printing of money can see huge changes in prices on a daily basis. So, our digital FutureGoldCoin will provide stability and predictability in the economy and a quick way to adjust that.

Secondly;

All countries can manipulate our currency to lower the value of their currency to boost exports. They can limit the amount of circulating currency of our FutureGoldCoin currency by holding our money in their country's reserves. When our money is scarce in their economy, this increases the value of our money but lowers the value of their local currency against ours. This makes their goods cheaper and this boost exports as more people would buy goods in their national currency's value. This is a positive tool to fight hyperinflation.

Thirdly;

All nations will increase the value of their own people as they print money. Whenever a government prints money they owe their citizens this newly printed money. But when they borrow money through loans from e.g. the World Bank or the IMF, they increase the value of external bodies and there is a huge risk as well if they default. Our methods ensure that all nations will keep printing new fresh money thereby increasing the value of their people. Our system will encourage governments to put the people first rather than now when the governments prioritize banks in return of names and addresses of the defaulters whom they buy into secret captivity where they end up illegally tagged and loaded with identifying watermarks through viruses and digital agents. The current system is to bail-out thieves in terms of banks. The banks stole $billions in mis-sold PPI a pre-planned trickery plan and the government in exchange for names and addresses bail-out these banks. Imagine the CEO of a company embezzling small funds over the years? Do you think when caught out he will walk free? Only the banks can steal and get away with it. Imagine all the educated cream of society in all banks making mistakes that cost the customers $40 billion in PPI insurance? Imagine a governed body like a bank that is answerable to the Financial Conduct Authority not following their own procedures of apply the PPI insurance and the loans that followed and still remain licensed when there is proof [in PPI returns in tunes of $billions] that they not only mis-sold but tricked everyone and promised the government a cut and still getaway? Trust me the system is now obsolete useless. Anyway, our system will make it mandatory to treat banks as banks government by any laws and not some protected-special-privileged entity. This makes banks answerable to us and we reward the people who put the government in power in the first place.

d. The government will and must bail-out the people first.

Fourthly;
Using our Futuregoldcoin will mean increased wealth of all nations. All nations will have what is free and fast money through printing the only way life intended. We have a system to tackle issues related to the printing of money like the hyperinflation, corruption, problems to create manufacturing, to meet the demand created by the new money, stagnating economies, flooding the markets, etc. Our system will hold every nation's own money in our Global Reserve Bank. Every nation will go from being in debt to having global savings. There is always money for everything. Countries can buy at market prices the only thing that separates them is their skills in manipulating fiscal measures. We as the global leader will and must level the playing field. We give every nation on earth a fair way to increase wealth to new heights. Our Global Reserve Bank will have deposits in all currencies and the countries will

get the equivalent in our currency that will start as a digital to fight hyperinflation. In later stages, this can have a supporting fiat system.

e. Every nation will and must have to use two currencies in their economies to steer growth.

i. Their own currency.

We believe in sovereignty and we will not take that away from any nation and this means each, and every country has its own currency just like now. They can still use their own currency but because of the problems of hyperinflation, they MUST use our digital money as well.

ii. The FutureGoldCoin.

They must use our FutureGoldCoin; a digital currency. Every nation will have to deposit their currency as collateral and in exchange, we will give them our own currency the equivalent or percentage of the newly printed money. This they must inject into their economy and use this for setting prices, etc.

Advantages of using our FutureGoldCoin.

The advantages are many;

They can tackle price fluctuations.

They can manipulate their own currency to have a competitive advantage and steer growth. They can trade globally cheaply at lower fees using our money.

Benefit greatly from the ever-increasing value of our FutureGoldCoin.

Above all our currency will be the New Single Reserve Global Currency meaning all nations will have to use this currency if they are to print and deal with the hyperinflation.

That will increase the value of our currency universally making it a powerful currency with ever-increasing value.

To be able to boost exports they must limit circulating supply of our money the Futuregoldcoin and if they don't, they will not be able to sell and that can see their businesses and companies going out of business because of a lack of the markets.

They must limit only circulating supply but must hold a load of our money as an investment as well as the value of our money will keep rising with every printing of money. Holding our money in large quantities but in their reserves will lower the value of their currency as compared to our Futuregoldcoin. So, exports become cheaper for international countries. So, this boosts their economies at the same time increasing the value of our currency globally. Every nation can trade and buy goods easily as our currency will be in use globally that increases trade without worrying about the exchange rates, etc.

Since we will hold all nation's currencies as savings, we can easily collect money from every nation say a percentage of the deposited savings to stimulate growth and provide services each country would not otherwise afford to.

We can increase global demand and markets;

We can increase high-quality infrastructure provisions.

We can create jobs globally as we can elect companies like multi-nationals who can say build new airport modern ones in areas which are forests now. Every country has land that is lying unused somewhere.

As a global leader and through the Global Reserve Bank we can initiate global new city development projects building new cities from stretch using this to deal with increased new money as the printing of money is continuous with few breaks in between.

We will have enough valuable money to build new cities, brand new airports, new roads, schools, etc. in areas that are woodlands now.

This is the only way to increase wealth and quality of life to the levels never seen before. No offense to the preservation of old buildings, these can remain. The new money is for new cities from stretch.

We through our Global Reserve Bank can link the whole globe through effective railway, new airplanes, consider all military aircraft converted for private use with everyone owning a jet, etc.

We'll have the money to pay royalties for clever inventions and use some inventions tied say in military-only-circles for the benefit of all humanity.

We will be able to ban getting expensive loans that only act to destroy the already accumulated wealth. The IMF and the World Bank must adjust or cease to operate with it emphasizes Economic structural adjustment programs and austerity measures. We will be able to provide free to low-cost loans that are safeguarded with printed own currency that acts as collateral. Our rationale is that as long as a country is sovereign it will have the right to print own money freely and cheaply. **Trust as a word of mouth that will revolutionize borrowing and the world.**

Every sovereign nation will have the right to print fresh new money. This is central to our system. This means that their word of mouth to pay from printed money becomes very solid that just that word and the promise to print and pay will be enough collateral for us as the world leader to start projects without receiving any money. This enables us to build say a city from stretch and complete it in less time namely a fraction of what it will take if we were to wait for deposits and payment. We can offer any services on being given a word of mouth and a promise to pay. This will revolutionize development and wealth and living standards. We can build a city in months; we have the money and a system that makes that perfect.

Our motto.

Our motto in this area is that only new money can increase wealth and growth, and this is not loan-money but only printed fresh money.

f. Our currency as the only New Single Reserve Global Currency.

Nations will use two or more currencies, but it is a must that they must use their own currency to gain a competitive advantage as they can easily manipulate their own currency to steer growth. Secondly, they must use our digital currency the FutureGoldCoin in that this is the buffer against hyperinflation. These two are a must but they can use their own digital as well as other countries' currencies, but this is discouraged as hyperinflation will destroy that economy. If using another countries currency like the US$ as the reserve currency problems will persist and this might diminish the growth of one country as for example the US might feel cheated, and if this is uncontrolled might lead to dirty tricks and or even wars. Our laws ban acts that can incite wars or make others think about starting a war so to correct the situation.

We encourage all nations to use our FutureGoldCoin as the only New Single Reserve Global Currency for the sake of peace. Using our currency as the NSRGC has so many benefits that the benefits will outweigh any disadvantages. Our currency which will be held in individual nation's reserves will be the global currency. All transactions will be carried out in our currency as the main currency. That means fast and cheaper transactions globally. Every country to beat hyperinflation must devalue their own country's currency in favor of ours to make their exports cheaper and boost exports and local manufacturing of goods and services. They must reduce the circulating currency of our currency holding some in their own reserves in their country. This is the only way to do it since they are printing money using their own money will devalue their money and destroy any development. So, they must use our currency as the main digital currency to set up prices as prices fluctuate many times a day due to the increased demand and circulating money. All of this will only increase the value of our money. This will encourage holding even more of our money in their reserves. In the end, our money will be the most valued. The fact that we trade our money with every countries' currency that makes our money the most prominent and widely used and to make things even better we don't belong to any nation even the US will benefit as they can do exactly what China etc. are doing right now to make their exports cheaper. This eliminates the Beggar-thy-Neighbor, the Triffin Dilemma issue and the development of a one big parasite country that relies on all other nations being poor in order for it to grow. All countries have equal opportunities to accumulate wealth and become a superpower through trade and development. We as a global leader level all the playing fields for them to realize just that. This, in the long run, will work well towards global peace and it encourages competition with nations competing with each other increasing wealth and development.

Nations can manipulate our currency to their own advantage locally in a country they can buy e.g. rights to control even our currency to their advantage. If one country suffers no other country can be dragged with it. The current system of using the US$ as the reserve currency means whatever the US suffers, they will drag all nations down with them. This is because the money being used by a nation as a reserve is the currency of another and whatever their economic or fiscal policies are these will impact the second nation using their currency.

The main argument against the current system is the fact that since all other countries are using another country's currency as a reserve that the country can easily destroy everyone's accumulated wealth within a flash.

For example, say if China over the years has been trading and accumulating wealth in US$ using the US$ as the reserve country. If the money accumulated for argument's sake is now $1000 000 the US overnight can print a large amount of their new money and inject this in the economy and what this does if lower the value of the US$. Overnight China's $1000 000 accumulated wealth can lose value overnight from a strong $1000 000 to nothing. So, this is putting your savings in someone's hands and to be honest in the hands of an enemy or competitor with only one result; destruction of your wealth in a flash.

This is what has been happening for decades with wealth accumulated only to be destroyed overnight and the process started again no wonder we still have the same issues seventy years ago when the Bretton Woods was implemented before it crashed.

Our system guarantees wealth to all forever and increased wealth for that matter as our money can only increase in value. Above all the countries' wealth will not be lost overnight just because another country printed money. Value is guaranteed for a long time. You can plan to know that even in the future your wealth is guaranteed and secure. Welcome to Tomorrow's World Order ladies and gentlemen, boys and girls.

Our system provides a robust strong system that is fit-for-purpose and safe and eliminates global crises and financial crises like 2008.

First;
We have laws to deal with unscrupulous nations that rob others because they are very educated than others and above all, they are the ones who created the current system and it only benefits themselves and no one else. Our system levels the playing field eliminating loopholes and bottlenecks that stales or can be used to crush the system. Our system is for all nations and mankind. The rationale behind our system is that of making mankind do what he is supposed to do; to be the best and operate above optimal levels.

I argued in my book: **Tomorrow's World Order** that we are not operating at our best. For the past 2000 years, we were stuck in the defensive system wasting resources using weapons to get all the expensive resources we can't afford in the process, killing innocent women and children. But I declared that this is because mankind as a whole has failed to think and take guts to do what is right. Instead, mankind has chosen the easy simple way; with the resources he had, he made weapons and used the weapons to get the expensive resources like oil at force through wars, invasions, sanctions, and assassinations. But years ago, when mankind had no option and lacked new methods to create wealth to levels never seen before that could be justified. But I have devised a method that works and what would be the excuse of continuing with cheaper easy methods yet the most destructive ones killing innocent yet precious people in any given society.

I declared that there can never be an excuse ever again, I have written new laws especially the E-Laws to squash such evil thinking with severe punishment most of which that involve death through our justice system, of course. This is because such practices are not just barbaric and evil but threatens the fabric of any society. If we can't defend these; the women and children, the only people who actually need help and to be defended who can we ever defend? So, our system provides peace and security for all through the elimination of financial crisis, this system empowers every nation to afford to buy any resources at market prices. This eliminates reliance on fossil fuels like oil as now every nation can afford to fund a strong research and development project into alternate renewable energy sources. There is money to invest in other areas and come up with alternatives in all areas. Instead of sending people to war they can make trade deals buying almost anything at market prices. Instead of other countries spending their money on defense fearing to be attacked causing hardships to their people the main reasons used as justification for wars. Instead they can afford to correct the issues raised by the rebels who they end up gassing using chemical weapons. They can afford to eliminate basic needs the main reasons cited by rebels to cause an uprising. Now they can form partnerships with the rebels and solve the problems. Now they don't care about the sanctions levied on them. They have the money and means to find an alternative. Our laws ban all these dirty tricks. No woman and child can die without the people responsible; facing our laws. This looks like a perfect system. Even if the country is failing, we have their deposits in our Reserve Bank, even if they don't have. All we need from them is *their word and promise to settle the debt through a cheaper guaranteed way; simply printing their own currency* which we can hold for them as collateral and even give them our currency the FutureGoldCoin to use. Everyone, in the end, is richer and in a better position even if they are bottlenecks and problems, we might not see we have enough money from all countries in our Global Reserve Bank to do something about it. Above all we are sovereign too in our own right. We can print and mint our own digital currency and is ready at the time of writing and can be improved if needed be. In the future we can have our fiat money to supplement the digital money. We have the power and money to build cities from stretch we shall build fast and take humanity to another level of life. In the end, our plans are to take all humanity to Networking and Cooperation stage where we are all one big people working together to improve humanity. You waste time fighting and creating boundaries when a lot still waits to be discovered and achieved wasting resources on the military to kill each other? Humanity?

g. Wages and Salaries.

Banning of taxes on income is a major step towards empowering everyone. The money you work hard for is all yours. You get all the money but you might find a small percentage taken towards personal government-held savings account one which they will use to assess eligibility and how much in loans etc. they can give you depending on a number of years worked which are to be regarded as contributions to the economy. This contribution can and might be doubled or tripled by the government depending on other criteria. This will only be used to assess and view this as collateral to be held so that they can release loans to you in case you are in difficulties. In no circumstances can savings be used for debt, etc.

New laws to put a safety net to protect savings and wealth. Wages and salaries will increase ideally cumulatively in that your salary must increase continuously in relation to time and not experience alone, etc. A certain percentage must be added to your wages and salaries say quarterly and in the end on a monthly basis. This is because goods and services increase more often. In our system, the value for money of goods and services will increase all the time that means prices might go up more often to match the value-added so wages and salaries must go up regardless of every quarter after some time monthly to reflect inflation. There must be a time when salaries and wages [as a proportion] will go up every month.

h. Savings.

I have already dealt with savings. Wealth and its creation the main cornerstone of our system must be protected, safeguarded, maintained and increased all the time to levels never dreamt of. So, savings play a central role in that, savings must be protected as mandatory. The government has a duty to protect individual savings no matter what. Savings must not be used for servicing debt, etc. The idea is to generate new money to pay for everyday consumables etc. and expenditure. We have new laws and a system that forbids debt and encourages a country's saving account. Likewise, we shall put new laws or encourage individual nations to put laws to protect already accumulated wealth. The government must view themselves as there to serve the people. This means bailing-out people through loans that can be given through the individual savings account held by the government. The government instead of national insurances will collect savings money from wages which they will deposit into an individual's personal savings account which they shall hold. The person has no access to the money until it reaches a certain level or when the person reaches a certain age. The government collects money from your wages and doubles or triples this money and in the end, the person will have access to this account. Whatever has been collected of the life span can and must be doubled or tripled by the government. In case of financial crises this account and its balance point to the government the level and amount of loan that can be offered in case the money is needed. The money remains with the government but used as collateral if it has not reached a certain amount level or if the person has not reached a certain age.

i. Governments to bail-out the people and not banks.

The government must not wait for the savings to be destroyed first in order to intervene. Local people of any country will be educated to seek government help etc. if they are in a difficult situation and if they have worked continuously for years, these savings can act as a collateral account. Wealth at the end of life must remain with the family and no government can claim and take the wealth of the deceased. Efforts to be carried out to hand the wealth to the close and even distant relatives as long as they are related. Donations of savings to charities and government bodies etc. e.g. hospitals are banned. We don't like a situation where people save-themselves to get the wealth, then when they get the wealth they realize that they run out of time and are all wrinkly and now they feel as if they have wasted their lives and give away the money to hospitals or charities who in most cases have robbed their youths for a monetary gain depriving them things when they have able-bodied only to die when they expect to enjoy their money. Guilty and shame making them give away this money even in some cases when they have families. This is wrong we consider this as grooming and if proven governments, institutions and charities can and might face criminal charges.

We believe this wealth must be passed to future generations. The current system encourages cycles of wealth followed by those of poverty and the cycle is repeated again, and again. The current system encourages the accumulation of wealth over a long period and only to lose that in a short period through a crisis, death or illness. Since most can be manipulated and the fact that most developed governments illegally tag or chip their citizens at birth, we regard it is and must be illegal for these governments and institutions to benefit. The existence of secret eugenics still in practice makes the whole system questionable and as such only banning these practices will benefit all. It is wrong for governments and it's institutions like the teaching hospitals the same people grooming the people who end up dead to do that for money illegal. We don't want cases where children have to take the government, charity or hospital to the court regarding wealth left by their parents. It is wrong. Savings belong and must stay within the family who might suffer the same disease due to genetic makeup so better cushion these rather than benefit the government who might have overused a radiation-emitting device with GPS properties the real trigger of the deceased's death. Criminal charges where it can be proved that the deceased was hacked and chipped by the government illegally or not without consent. No consent can be given by someone under the age of sixteen years without a parent, a guardian, etc.

j. Wealth in property and land.

New laws to protect property and land. No repossession for a certain period and the government to use the collected savings to bail-out individuals using this account as collateral. New rules to safeguard property rights etc. Banning of all taxes on individual property when buying property taxes can only apply when selling the property for profits. The buying process should not include any taxes especially if it is the only property for the family. The situation can change if it is a second house or buying to resale when already possessing another property. More powers to own and possess property and land. All young couples to be backed by the government to own property and land of their own. The government must use the collected savings [instead of national insurance] to assess affordability and suitability for mortgages and loans, etc. People who work often will have paid more into the savings account even if you have a lot of years in which they can contribute. The government to match or even double and triple this balance. The government must offer mortgages and long-term loans as long as these are for ownership of property and land. Mind you there will be enough printed money and the government must find ways of putting this money to use and this is one of those uses. For a small profit just to make the system fair and encourage good practices must offer mortgages and loans for a profit over time. Printing money will generate surplus money in the economy and our system acknowledges that the government must use this money to empower its people and increase, maintain and even increase further the wealth. The money must be put to good use otherwise the system will crash. Our system will encourage the huge infrastructure development making new cities from stretch. So new houses will replace the current dilapidated houses with poor building materials and energy-efficient properties. Modern buildings will save energy etc. and be fit for purposes. Quality will play a huge role. Provide high quality and people are more likely to pay more than normal. Banning of taxes, duties on property buying, etc. and even some selling if selling to upgrade must be exempt from government taxes.

k. Taxes and our system.

We aim to abolish taxes on income. The reasons now why governments collect taxes is because they have no other ways of raising income for maintaining services and to be able to provide services and build new infrastructure. To Tomorrow's world Order we think the current system is a mistake even though this is vital for the current system. Our system eliminates the need to collect taxes. All income will be free from all taxes. Yes, no taxes at all. We give back the people their money. Most of these people work very hard for their money only for the government to take all. We are against that. What you work for is all yours.

We are going to abolish taxes, but people will still pay a small percentage towards an individual-national-savings account. The current national insurance contribution will be used for a person's government savings account. All money deducted will be used to increase the balance of your government-held-savings account. You will not have access until at a certain age but it's all yours and the government will not take any and after the date might match what you have deposited as a refund of the 'I owe you' principle generated by it printing the new money. We shall make it a law that a percentage of the printed money is credited to each individual. Say, for example, a 0,001 percentage of printed money is given to each citizen as a share percentage and the equivalent recorded against that person. Over the years when that person gets into debt and can't pay that person must not use their savings to pay for the debt.
Savings once again to be protected by the law.
Instead, that person can approach the government and against this 'I owe you' balance claim, a loan or help with mortgage together with the money deducted as towards a national savings account will determine the amount that can be given by the government.
The government must view a certain percentage of the loaned money or mortgages as lost as in depreciation circles. A certain percentage must be considered as already lost from the beginning. Say as an example. Forty percent of all borrowed money must be considered as lost and a 'depreciation-like amount is set aside to account for that lost money. The idea is to increase the chances of everyone to accumulate wealth. But whatever a person can payback as part of the 'lost' money is welcome. If a person borrows $100 and can afford to repay all $100 that will be great but if they can pay e.g. back only $60, this is also good because at the start the government has set aside from the newly printed money $40 to act as lost -depreciated money'. In this case, the government will not have suffered any loss and the debt can be easily written off. The idea here as well is to fight individual, national and global debt and making the system realistic and not like the current system where global debt has risen to above $244 trillion. The system is now obsolete

hence our super system.

The system encourages working by the people but in a smarter way. There are incentives to go to work and better to start your own business as this will increase your collateral that means increased borrowing power and the better you will benefit assuming that for every hundred dollars you borrow if you meet a certain good standing character you will need to pay back only 60% of the funds. Working and employment will increase your assets being held by the government which it can use as collateral to give you loans, mortgages, etc.

How then will the government generate tax-equivalents?

No governments will collect income tax. Instead, all governments will print money to act just like the previously collected tax money. They can withdraw the equivalent of some of this money from our Global Reserve Bank. They can print this money and deposit all or a percentage with us where we offer our FutureGoldCoin equivalents that they can use to fund things they would normally fund with tax money. In turn, they can allocate a certain percentage of their deposit to us Tomorrow's World Order where through our multi-nationals we can provide such services they would normally pay with tax-sums of money. If it's for a new railway line, they can pay the multinationals or simply tell us what percentage of their deposit, we can use for providing this. They can simply withdraw money from us and do this on their own. We are not taking government responsibilities from them. We are simply providing a faster and cheaper way to see projects that would be normally done in years be done in months if not weeks. Through our Global Reserve Bank Development package.

1. Tomorrow's World Order's Global Reserve Bank Development Project [GRBDP].

We represent all nations and we will work for their best interests unlike bodies like the World Bank that are there just to collect and remove surplus money from the economy our GRBDP aims to provide fast and highest quality infrastructure and services globally. We aim to employ multinational companies in all areas who will build a city in months instead of years. They will have powers to buy land and or get permission through us to start huge projects creating jobs and offering supply and demand due to increased money. Printing money means a high demand as the people have the money to buy things and a quick way of providing high-quality services and infrastructure is a must. Why now countries fail using the printing money method is that they increase the money supply without equivalent high-quality infrastructure to match. People would not pay high prices for the infrastructure in place most of which have been there for decades. But if you build a new city from the stretch with modern expensive building people would pay high prices so the system is maintained because there is an equally expensive infrastructure or service to match and maintain the balance. Our huge multinationals will be able to build a rail network fast and increase the prices of the new system and not of the old system. The current system increases money and expect people to pay high prices for the poor dilapidated and out-of-date infrastructure or services. Human nature denies this, and people keep the money and the system will collapse as no one will pay for such services.

We can provide such services fast at a discount as we already hold their services and, in most cases, to fight hyperinflation, we can provide the services with nothing to pay now say pay in five years, etc. The ability of the government through its sovereign status will make us take a word for them to pay as collateral. The system relies on Trust and because of the sovereignty of all nations, we can take their word for it.

A word of mouth becomes more solid and valuable than gold the way it is intended.

Why should they not pay-up when they can print in a flash? For now, to get a loan, you must have a good debt record and some assets like government bonds, etc. Our system can establish faith and trust as it was originally intended had the principles of global wealth and governance have been best understood.

m. Trust as a deposit something that will revolutionize borrowing.

Our system makes borrowing fast and safe as nations can borrow from Tomorrow's World Order huge loans against only a word of printing and depositing this money with us. The current system does not allow that in that heavy printing will only devalue that currency leading to the crashing of the system. But our system ensures that the value is maintained as the new money is deposited in savings accounts with our Global Reserve Bank. So, all a government need is **the promise to print and pay us at a future date** taking into consideration inflation, etc. and the promise to deposit the amount with us and pay over years. There is trust again in the system in that we can, without doubt, believe that to be true. Their money will still be valuable to us in years to come. We can initiate the projects right away without even receiving a cent from the nation concerned this just being built on trust and a system that encourages that. Development is faster we can build brand new modern airports, cities, megapolises, buildings, railways, new planes, connecting the whole world fast in months if not weeks as we have the resources something that a government or nation can take years to build and accomplish. So, our system simplifies everything. Above all this eliminates the need for big lenders like the USA having to make and possess nuclear weapons to use as their guarantee that they will get back their loaned-money the main reason or justification used for the few nations to make and keep nukes. We will only take their word for it and above all, they might have already deposited a certain percentage in our Global Reserve Bank that we can use as collateral. As long as they are sovereign, we will know they will fulfill their obligation and pay us. This is the only way to increase wealth to levels we can only dream of. Using the same system or thinking we can offer cheaper loans or simply money that can be used for what would have been used with the tax money.

n. Dealing with the individual, national and global debt.

We have a system in place that is against the debt of any kind which will grow to unmanageable levels. We from the start will try to negotiate all debt and encourage everyone to do the same. Incentives are given to clear current debt and encouraging those owed to reduce and write off the debt. No point keeping debt for decades you are sure that will never be paid. We shall and must treat debt as a depreciating asset just like a car that depreciates with time. So initially one loan provider, a bank, a nation or institution will have to make provisions for the defaulted value that is lost loans due to non-payments. The percentages must be high. If the government maybe 50% should be set aside for the bad debt. So, you will only expect back 50% of the money loaned out. So initially you set aside a provision for bad debt with 50% of the money deposited into this debt account. So, if a person fails to pay the 50% the money is transferred from this provisional account to the loan account to make the balance initially loaned out.

It is our responsibility to contact and deal with debt encouraging writing off of this debt especially if the debt is of a certain age. The older the debt, the lower the value of that debt. We assume that over the years the value of the debt has depreciated and therefore written off. Say all debt over, for example, ten years if loans, etc. can be reduced, negotiated or written off. This is not the loans' duration. This is the debt that has not been paid after the agreement was canceled due to nonpayment. This does not apply to loans to be repaid in 20 years, etc. This is only when a person can't pay back such loans. We aim to free people from debt, so they are able to save and accumulate wealth after that. There shall never be a consideration of debt after the writing off has expired. The writing-off period must and shall never be more than two years. After that, a person can and will start afresh. But this can be related to the amount of the written-off debt. The more the debt the more the waiting or writing-off period. Once the debt is written off the government is not to hassle and harass the individual that once was in debt nor will they secretly enslave that person by getting him or her tagged illegally so that they can intimidate, torture or degrade inhumanly that person. Severe punishment to nations doing this holding everyone to ransom offering illegal loans to hold the people and control them.

The same applies to us Tomorrow's World Order too, we shall not hold any nations to ransom who we have cleared of owing us after the writing-off period has expired. No will we monitor their activities after that. Over the first five years, nations are expected to be debt-free and with huge savings in our Global Reserve Bank. That will eliminate global, national and individual debt. We will negotiate all global debt and or buy out this debt so that all nations start afresh for the new system to take effect.

o. Tax and infrastructure maintenance.

Our system acknowledges that there won't be a need to collect taxes from the income of people. Since we are printing money and to drive the economy new money will be printed for activities current dealt with the tax money. Money for tax purposes is printed and sent to a certain tax account and there is no need to deposit this with us, Tomorrow's World Order in our Global Reserve Bank. This money is fresh money and can be injected directly into the economy where it is needed. This is the money used for salaries, wages, servicing of infrastructure and other daily activities. The level of service they provide will determine how much they will collect as service level fees. Individuals will still have to pay for services say government buildings, houses, services, facilities, etc., transport systems, etc. The fee to be paid will be in relationship to the quality. We as Tomorrow's World order shall introduce a value for the service system in that for services and infrastructure that meets a certain grade the government or responsible body can charge a higher fee. So, the better the quality the higher the money they can collect. We shall vet and grade services and infrastructures so every nation, city or council can set their own prices according to the quality of the services. Those who do not meet certain levels will be dragged to our justice system to be punished. It is illegal to provide poor standards of services and infrastructure.

p. Source of money for maintaining services and infrastructure.

Our aim is to continuously provide services and high-quality infrastructure all the time and the only secure guaranteed source is through a percentage of the printed money. The current issues are that money collected is reinvested into service provisions just like the current political system this is wrong in that the money plowed back into the maintenance is dependent on the quality of service. That means for decades you will never increase the funds over a certain percentage of the money raised. Even if it's 90% of the collected money is plowed back into maintenance, this is related to the money paid for the service. This can only mean the same or slightly better standards over the years. Our system relies on a percentage of printed money to be used for the maintenance of infrastructure and services. This percentage will grow annually which means there is always money for maintenance not related to the amount they charge for the service nor on how much is collected. This can only mean increased quality of services. This system means any collected money can be used to spicy up further the infrastructure and service provision as the collected money is extra money that can be plowed back.

q. Role of the government in relation to wealth.

It is a mandatory duty of a government or nation to serve their people as per our new laws. Every government exists to serve its people. This means aiming to increase the wealth of its people. Every time a government prints new fresh money it owes its people. This derives from the laws of bookkeeping where a balance must have a debit and a credit transaction. Printing new money increases the value of people. So, the government must protect the value and wealth of the people. The government has a mandatory obligation to protect the wealth of its people. They must safeguard savings and people's investments. Every care must be taken to protect the wealth of the people. The economy is designed in such a way that it must print money and put this money in the economy. This increases growth and demand and there will come a time when the new money will increase activities that require even more money from the people. At one point the money in the economy will shrink and the people will find themselves unable to pay e.g. to repay for loans, mortgages, etc. at this stage it is the government's duty to act and bail-out the people. The current system waits until the people have used up their savings and lost everything even then the current system priorities the banks and would rather bail-out the banks than ordinary people. Our system will make it a mandate to bail-out the people through cheaper loans, mortgages, etc. directly offered by the government or on behalf of the government. The rationale behind such bailout is that initially when the government printed the new money it created an 'I owe you' to its people. This is now the time to pay that 'I owe you note' by bailing-out the people through cheaper loans and mortgages, etc. These loans and mortgages will have to be written-off or a percentage of this written off over a time period. A government can use a merit scheme to write off these loans for those who might find it hard to pay off the loans. It is a crime for governments to let their people lose their own savings when it comes to help and bail-out the people. This will see continuous increases in wealth. The current system lets people save over the years and only to lose everything in a flash and then to start again.

r. Our systems and savings.

We advocate for an increase in global wealth to levels never seen before. The current system lets people save money over the years for the savings to be destroyed in a flash and the whole process started again. Our system put laws and regulations to avoid that. Savings will be protected by our laws. The government in cases of the crisis must provide a rescue package. Cases like as in the 2008 financial crisis are against what we stand for. Governments must act proactively and print new money to deal with debt especially if widespread as in 2008. Already accumulated wealth must be protected. For over 200

years humanity has been growing wealth at low levels and only this to be destroyed. Our system shall and must take wealth levels to new heights. We have laws to protect wealth as governments must:
protect savings,
bail-out citizens instead of bailing-out banks,
offer cheaper easily available loans and mortgages,
to write off debt or buy-out this debt to write it off at a later date;
must always recognize as being there to serve the people and this means do everything in its power to increase wealth, protect the wealth already obtained, intervene to save the people and not to wait until there is a crisis, put laws punishing rather than licking corrupt banks and institutions, eliminate bureaucracy that stifles anything that helps wealth accumulation, must always use the 'I owe you' generated by the printing of new money to do things that enhance the wealth and living standards of its people.

s. Governments must put things in place to ensure the continuous accumulation of wealth.

Empower every human being and increase national and personal wealth to levels never achieved or dreamt of before.
We are against austerity measures and will not accept the current system as the best we can achieve. We as Tomorrow's World Order, strongly believe that we are working way-below our optimal or best levels. There is room for growth, and we have the system, laws, rules, and regulations to boost the wealth of every nation and human being to levels only dreamt of. Our system works and we shall put laws to punish nations who practice austerity measures at the expense of their people. We as Tomorrow's World Order strongly believe that all governments exist only to serve the people. The current system gives a lot of power to the government who in turn makes laws that suppress the people who elected them in power in favor for example of other institutions like banks. This is wrong. Governments must bail-out the people and not banks as the current thinking. Banks steal literally from the people and are given immunity by the

governments who gain also as they buy the people's rights and freedom of all those who defaulted getting these tagged and controlled to drive the government services and institutions speaking of modern-day slavery and gross human rights abuses. Governments exist to serve the people just like we exist to serve all nations making sure that they are wealth and better off. Our system shall and must-see every nation on earth increase its wealth exponentially, wealth that will trickle down to the people.

t. The government has a duty to make sure that wealth is passed from generation to generation.

The current system is unfair and discourages the wealth to be passed from generation to generation. One generation works very hard for years accumulating wealth which they will all lose to the government. This is wrong and must be corrected. Wealth must be continuously be passed on from one generation to the other. Our aim is to increase wealth to levels never seen before and the current system robes hard-working generations by keeping the wealth that is unclaimed as lost possibly as relatives die too. That can encourage the government to illegally tag and deliberately kill those very rich whose wealth they can end up inheriting. That can explain the secretive eugenics movements that are used as reasons to deny certain people the ability to have their own children. Therefore, our system bans; the
passing of wealth unclaimed to the government after all relatives had died.
It is and will be illegal to donate your wealth to the government or to a charity. Many people work very hard all their life accumulating wealth and only to die of a disease and then donate all their wealth towards that disease. We stand against this because if this helped over the past seventy years, we will have achieved a lot to eradicate such diseases but even now the diseases then are still the same diseases killing people now. So, we ban donations to any institutions like the hospitals of terminally ill people to other government institutions and charities of one's wealth. This is a law and is illegal and most

people who donate in their last days of death do so when they are weak and have suffered dementia etc. and weaken by the havoc of diseases that they would end up giving away their wealth towards a disease that killed them neglecting their families, etc. No individual wealth to be donated to organizations and the government. All wealth must and will remain in the family of the deceased. If no relatives are found even, then no funds will and must end up in the government coffers instead this is the money that can be distributed for good cause to charities and only if there is no suitable relative. Our reasoning is this. If a person has families and disease kills that person giving money to charities or government who have taken money for the past seventy years still with no tangible results is a waste of precious money. We acknowledge that relatives have a chance of suffering the same disease etc. due to genes and it will be sound thinking to leave all wealth with relatives giving them a better chance of fighting the disease. We believe that the current system encourages the government to employ dirty tactics making sure that they will benefit in the end from the wealth when the person dies. The fact that most people since the 1940s are illegally tagged at birth without consent and the same medical devices designed to protect them becoming the ones used to kill them directly or indirectly through radiation as they use radiation and GPS properties, etc. This can be regarded as grooming by the governments for a price; the wealth when all die and the radiation making most infertile so as not to leave offspring. We don't reward wrongdoing and as such, it is against our laws even if the person is willing to donate their wealth or part to charity or government. Our laws will take effect and care to be taken to look for relatives even distance relatives as long as they can prove a relationship to the deceased. In no circumstances will the government take unclaimed wealth. This is the money that will fund good causes in cases where there are no close or distant relatives found.

u. Increase life's longevity and improve the quality of life.

Our aim is to prolong life in the youth stages and improve the quality of life. Research and development to spearhead the drive to improve life. The current system encourages government and leaders to make all kinds of dirty-weapons; viral, digital and recently cyber weapons that are used as watermarks on people say a form of protection, etc. in other countries causing severe deformities and alignments, in the end, killing these people. Some countries buy loans and mortgages defaulters from banks by bailing-out banks and then use watermarks in the form of viral and digital agents to control and monitor these defaulters. In other countries especially without the death penalty, the governments are loading their people with these watermarks as an alternative to the death sentence or other punishment. In the end, people end up being framed, and the method used as a tool to control the people. We as Tomorrow's World Order strongly are against the making of bio-engineered, digital or cyber weapons for any reason. We stand against the loading of humans with any of these for any reason being it watermarks, etc. Some countries still practice secret eugenics watermarking their people with deadly viruses as a way of preserving these and their way of life, but all this is leaving their people with gross health issues lowering the life span and the quality of life. Our aim and goals are to increase life span through research and development, education and our justice system. Funding must be set aside to find how we can prolong life in youth and improve the quality of life. It is illegal to load people with harmful agents; viral, bio-engineered or digital, etc. Chipping of people with secret devices that are remotely operated for any reason is banned simply because these uses and emits radiation that kills. Any such an act is regarded as a murder act. It is as good as killing that person so stiff sentences, especially where governments illegally and secretly especially at birth implant these Medical Implanted Devices that are remotely operated with GPS properties. Very stiff sentences to governments who do this especially to certain racial groups like the mixed-races where they are controlled remotely through the local councils and other government apparatus like the teaching hospitals and police where they are abused remotely through electromagnetic stimulation where an electrode is inserted at birth and a rotary propeller used to control behavior, etc. We strongly are against human hacking because the aim of a hacker is to change, modify, damage, control, and in the end cause malfunctions. So, a hacker who is in effect a torturer is worse than a slave trader and a killer hence our death punishment laws against human hacking. See in ***Filártiga v. Peña-Irala,*** it was noted that; Indeed, for purposes of civil liability, the torturer has become like the pirate and slave trader before him Hostis Humani Generis, an enemy of all mankind.

Our laws, rules, and regulations take a holistic approach to improve life and the quality of life as well as providing a framework to protect a nation's or individual's life through the right to self-defense. New laws banning wars that kill most innocent women and children. Banning invasions that lower quality of life and threatens the lives of innocent people. Banning the viewing of women's and children's lives as collateral damage. Banning acts that interfere with quality of life. Poor infrastructure provisions can see the government and councils be punished by our system. Banning reliance on fossil fuels that pollute the air we breathe lowering the life-span and quality of life. Banning poor housing materials etc. Establishing minimum standards globally. Bring some governments to justice for prioritizing the economy's balance sheet at the expense of their people.

v. Take humanity out of the defensive stages of development.

The defensive stage has become obsolete now evidenced by a lack of major global wars and now it is a huge waste to invest huge sums in the military and in defense. Above all, we as Tomorrow's World Order strongly believe that even if the defensive stage was and is still relevant, the weaponry is now obsolete. A few countries are making cyber, digital weapons, etc. that can wipe-out all humanity without even going to war or using current weaponry. So, investing in weaponry is a waste especially considering that $1,7 trillion per year [2017] is being channeled on weapons manufacturing and the military at the expense of other areas. Humanity cannot afford to be stuck in the defensive stages where the thinking is to make weapons cheaper and then use these weapons to gather the more expensive resources like oil cheaper through force, wars, sanctions, invasions, elimination of leadership of countries with oil resources, and dirty tricks, etc. For 2000 years mankind has been doing the same thing we are saying that is not only obsolete and wrong but barbaric as well and a crime to be punished harshly through our justice system. We as the global leader has a mandatory duty to take all nations out of the defensive stages of development. We will ban all things making humanity be stuck in defensive stages; these include wars, weapons manufacturing, possession, selling, and dealings, etc. We shall ban reliance on fossil fuels the trigger for most global wars. We shall ban sanctions and other dirty tricks. We strongly believe as Tomorrow's World Order that all current and possibly future global problems are a result of a lack of affordability. We believe that mankind has failed to think outside the box and as such relies on the defensive stage as a driver of the economy. Making cheaper weapons and using these and wars to drive the economy getting expensive resources they can't afford by force through wars, sanctions, and invasions, etc. We shall, therefore, provide a system that is a solution to all this. A system that will increase global wealth so that every nation can afford to buy resources at market price. This will and must eliminate humanity's reliance on weapons for everything. This will take humanity out of the defensive system to the next stage of development; Networking and Cooperation.

w. Health

Health is important on its own and central to our policies as we aim to prolong life and improve quality of life. We have goals to take life and wealth to new levels never achieved before. The private -individual-government held savings account to act as a health collateral account. People don't pay tax and national insurance instead they contribute towards their personal savings account held by the government. The rate initially can be a single figure percentage of their wages which is collected and deposited into their savings account. This is used as a way to assess the amount to provide loans etc. health insurance or cover, mortgages, etc. but most importantly this will act as collateral for health cost. They are expected to deposit a certain amount into this account to qualify for free health. The idea is to make people contribute to a lesser extend to things that matter to them the most that way there is a sense of responsibility on their part to contribute and act and live healthily. The government is responsible to provide health for those who have contributed to the savings account. A scheme can be in place to encourage savings to be channeled to this government-held savings account. We want a system where people contribute even a small part to the things that are central to them. This as well ensures that the government is not tempted to try to watermark the people making viruses, bio-engineered or digital ones as a fee for free service provisions while testing these on people. The countries where there is a free health system these countries have secret watermarking of people, etc. related to eugenics movements and to safeguard and preserve the people and most are conservatives. These governments make viruses in all forms, bio-engineered or now digital which are used to control and even test viruses on these people. So be careful about what is free. As long as they have for example $1000 in their government-held savings account they are entitled to free health. The governments don't take their hard-earned money in taxes, but we encourage everyone to contribute to their savings account until there is at least $1000 balance. This is their money the government will keep until the amount has reached a certain amount, for example, $10 000 or if the person has reached a certain age where they have an excess to that savings account. This savings account will act as collateral for the government to provide a lot of everything health, loans, mortgages, certain housing, etc. I believe in free health for all, but we need people to show they understand that life is central to everything we stand for and this means everyone doing something about things that are critical for their survival. I don't want to see exchanges associated with free things. There are no free things in life. People tend to take care if they contribute towards the issue. If life matters a $1000 means nothing and sacrificing this towards one's savings account will work to motivate the people to live healthily as well. Most free service has always had a catch. Better save the $1000 which is yours in the end anywhere and avoid being loaded with viral watermarks in exchange for the free service. I encourage accountability and responsibility. I want to build people that have high self-esteem. A people who understand that free things are not free. To me, free things represent doing nothing. If we do nothing, we are never going to achieve anything. If we do nothing, we are never going to increase our self-esteem. Imagine a body not exercised or trained that body has many issues in the long run than when a person walks a day a few miles, minutes, etc. contributing to the things that matter. The $1000 acts as a reminder as well for people to act to live healthily. The health is free for all but a deposit of $1000 guarantees everyone excesses to free health.

Those who can't afford etc. can simply get free health as long as they can prove they can't. But this must be compulsory to all with those who can afford to encourage to do so but still in possession of its savings account. The government will pay for everything because our policies are to save wealth and for this to remain in the family. I believe the health sector and your governments have become trickery and devious using illegal hacking at birth to gain a competitive advantage and control the destiny of people making people save wealth only to lose all in a flash. We advocate for the preservation of wealth within the family. The free health care policies have left people exposed to abuse and grooming by the teaching hospitals. Treated as cash-cows to be harvested losing everything in a flash and some ending up donating all their wealth to hospitals and charities, etc.

When it comes to health, I think health insurance is not good for the majority instead the government must use the savings account to collect the savings from pay and then get health insurance to all its citizens itself but offer health to all using this savings account as collateral. Using these savings account then provides enough money to cover health costs. The government can pay for all health costs as long as the cost doesn't exceed a certain amount as an example say $10 000. If the cost exceeds that, then the government pay says 95% if above say $15 000 the government pays only 90%, etc. The balance say 5% if cost exceeds $10 000 and 10% if cost exceeds $15 000 is debited to the savings account to reduce the balance but after 5 years had elapsed, the amount is credited back as the money is written off by the government as long as the person has kept contributing towards the savings account.

Our policies aim and put a mandatory requirement on the government to do everything it can to save the wealth already in the hands of the people. The government must directly be responsible for the payment of the health of its people. Those who can afford to go private can but are still required to contribute towards the savings account with the government. For most no one shall lose the already wealth accumulated when they become sick, etc.

There are many policies and underlying principles to cover but this volume will cover these fundamental principles only.

4 OUR AIMS AND OBJECTIVES IN SHORT;

To provide strong leadership to the whole globe.

To provide a guiding, spearheading and an overseeing role in that we act as a catalyst to speed up and lead processes necessary and fundamental to global growth, peace and security.

To provide a foundation and framework that lays the laws, rules, and regulations to be followed and adhered to by all mankind under the sun.

To provide rules and regulations to be followed by all nations and institutions.

To lay down rules, monitor these, enforce these and bring perpetrators to justice.

To provide a legal and justice system that is effective globally for the sake of the rule of law, upholding the rules regarding all humanity.

To write and amend global laws to be adhered to by all nations and all humanity.

To act as guiding leaders to all global leaders advising and acting on behalf of all global leaders for the sake of global peace and wealth.

To act as the global think tank, prescribing solutions to all global problems putting things in place to spearhead the development, global wealth to levels never seen before, peace, human rights, and development. Improving life globally.

To provide a financial system that boosts global wealth. We have the right to mint and print our own currency that will be used to empower all global nations.

To educate and advise all global nations.

4.1 To ensure that the basic prerequisites are met first and these are;

Empowering all nations and making sure that each and every nation is sovereign in its own right. Our system relies on all nations being sovereign. To provide laws, rules, and regulations that empower all nations and bringing violators to justice.

Putting down laws to remove things that interfere with the rights to a nation's sovereign e.g. by banning borrowing by nations that can see them lose their sovereignty if they fail to pay, etc.

To put down laws, rules, and regulations in relation to global infrastructure and living standards. Declaring minimum standards globally. Enforcing these and bringing perpetrators to justice.

To put down laws, rules, and regulations in relation to human rights, etc. Rules of which must be adhered to by all mankind under the sun.

To provide a framework and system that plans for the future. A system and framework that writes and impose rules, laws, and regulations to plan for the future through;

Banning wars.

Banning weapons manufacturing.

Banning huge investments in the military and defense.

Banning reliance on fossil fuels setting dates when fossil fuels will be banned.

Banning equipment, buildings, and vehicles that rely on and use fossil fuels, etc.

Banning killings of women and children,

Banning unnecessary killings or sacrificing of military personnel.

Banning dirty-tactics, false-flagging, sacrificing civilians as collateral damage, etc.

Banning links between governments and banks or financial institutions, etc.

Controlling all global governments making sure they adhere to our global laws, rules, and regulations.

Controlling institutions and making sure that they don't feed the current problems but act to solve the problems.

Limiting the life-span of the institutions making sure they operate and tackle a topic for a limited time frame rotating tasks etc. to make them effective.

Controlling financial institutions making sure that they don't rip-off the people and imposing tight punishments for these where they break their own rules and procedures to deceive and trick and steal from the ordinary people.

To remove current rules where banks are given immunity at the expense of the people together with the government conning people out of $billions and in the end selling the people who in most cases have defaulted on loans etc. as 'slave to the government' to steer or drive other departments. Very stiff laws.

To make rules, laws, and regulations and educate the nations that all governments exist to serve the people and not the other way round. So, the sole responsibility of a government is to serve its people and empower them to become very rich. To educate nations that people come first and as such governments are there to increase the wealth of the people who put them in power.

5. WHAT IS TOMORROW'S WORLD ORDER IN RELATION TO NATIONS?

We are not established to take over nations' governance, etc. We act as a global leader and as a national leader in the end as our members can become the leaders of nations but we don't intend to take over current or future national leadership illegally or by force but we aim to endorse candidates who will peacefully through the voting system and observing all laws win and take office so that our party will rule the world globally with representative leaders in every country. Current leaders and future ones will continue to run and govern their own nations with little or no interference from us as long as they don't do anything that conflicts with our universal laws or break these. Most of our rules are norms or common laws current in the current system. So, we are not introducing anything new or not known. We have rearranged the priority and emphasized other laws in that case all governments must make sure that they are up-to-date with our laws and act accordingly.

We don't aim to take over from current leadership even though our members might end up in the leadership roles of nations; this will only be because of the popularity of our laws, what we stand for and regulations. We intend to not directly impact how each nation is run unless if they are serial breakers of our laws.

6 OUR RELATION TO INSTITUTIONS AND SOME CHARITIES.

Just like any government, we don't interfere with the work of institutions, NGOs and charities, etc. but we have established regulations that they must follow. We saw it fit to limit the time periods institutions, NGOs and charities, etc. can be allowed to work on a subject matter. Most charities, institutions, etc. work on say human rights, poverty, torture, etc. for years, working to solve the issues central to their cause. We have decided that it is time to limit the number of years they can operate on a topic. We saw it fit to offer licenses or for the governments in areas, they operate to give them 5- year periods on a topic before moving to another related issue. The idea is to increase effectiveness and make sure they are not creating issues or not solving these so that they have a salary in the future. We need to give licensees to institutions and organizations that can work to solve the problems.

Firstly;

The main idea behind this is the risk of giving people a false sense of security that these institutions, NGOs or charities are there to help and solve issues when they are there just to safeguard a fat paycheck for their employees at the end of the month.

Secondly;

The issue relates to the fact that most rely on donations and wealth of the elderly that most end up receiving the wealth that is meant for relatives rather than them. Most rely on donations and we are strict with the destruction of the wealth and or getting the wealth of elderly people which is supposed to be meant for relatives hence the monitoring of these. So new laws to limit the period the institutions, charities, etc. work on a topic.

After 5-years an assessment can reveal if the license should be extended at least by two more years and if still doing well by a further two years. In which if all the years a total of nine years they had achieved a lot and done well to solve the problem and a further five years can be awarded on the same issue. For most 5 years should be enough. After the five years, they are expected to change focus and look at another topic and must apply for a new license for 5 five-year periods to work on the next topic. Licenses can be extended after 5 years if the charity, institutions, etc. did not source and receive donations from the elderly and in excess of a certain amount to be considered locally. An amount that can be given as donations by the elderly must be capped. New laws to make it hard for the elderly to give away their wealth. It must be considered incorrect for people to work all their life and then give away all their money to charity, institutions, etc.

This must be considered as abnormal unless if that person is very rich that the donated money is a fraction of the person's wealth. New laws to stipulate a percentage of the wealth that can be donated normally less than 1% of the wealth.
I have read of families fighting the government, institutions, and charities for the wealth donated to these institutions in some cases living nothing at all for their relatives. We will consider these cases as the elderly having been coerced to donate or be tortured to give away that money against their will. We must assume that age affects one's judgment and as such people must have the law on their side. To protect wealth and make sure wealth is passed from generation to generation we must monitor governments, institutions, NGOs and charities, etc.

7 CONCLUSION

I have so far dwelt much on what Tomorrow's World Order stands for and I am sure that this is a new way of thinking something never tried before but something I am sure will work and must work for us to achieve wealth levels never even imagined before. There is a way and we are the only ones with the solutions to all global problems.

Above all this is the only new method of doing things and we know the results of all the other alternatives as they are just new versions of the methods they tested and tried on for the past seventy years. I guaranteed you that choosing another political party with all their methods will only repeat what we as a people have been experiencing for the past seventy years since after the Second World War. How much time should we waste on obsolete systems and methods designed after the war and which are now obsolete and not for this day and age?

Would not it be a smart move to try a brand-new way of thinking?

A brand-new approach.

Above all what is not to like in;

Saving money, you sweated and hard-worked for through abolishing of payments of income tax and national insurance. What is not to like to have another savings account, imagine how much you pay in your life as taxes and national insurances and the value of what you get back? Imagine all that money being yours and no one else? Surely this is a huge step towards human emancipating and global wealth. The question is; Are you ready? I am.

What is not to like to have a health plan that will make sure you are 100% covered? Most of the people accumulate wealth for years sacrificing life to gather resources and only to lose these when they fall sick due to a lack of a plan like ours that protects the savings and let the greedy pharmaceutical companies who make deals with the government to benefit through letting the governments illegally tag everyone at birth. And over the years use radiation to remotely electromagnetically hack and change the course of life causing all kinds of diseases then let the pharmaceuticals jump in and provide medicines that don't last; wiping out all your savings and wealth before you die anywhere? Speaking of government led-grooming in the darkest meaning of the word. This is wrong. Our system will be proactive in fighting such acts where it matters at birth, making sure that no one is illegally tagged or remotely 'tortured' secretly, etc. We shall bring stiff death penalties to all human hackers; be it governments or not. No one is immune.

What is not to like when all your savings and wealth will increase the levels depending on your input forever? We have laws and systems to see to that.

What is not to like if all countries have brand new cities and high-quality infrastructure globally on top of the already existing system giving you an option of where to live depending on your disposable income?

Imagine a world without global financial crises, poverty and all bad things associated with a lack of affordability.

Imagine everyone having a say in things that matter to you? Our motto; Your Future Your Say is relevant here.

Imagine a world without wars, weapons and their possession and manufacturing.

Imagine a world without reliance on fossil fuels; the main trigger of all past wars?

Imagine a world with alternative cleaner and even cheaper energy sources?

Only our system will provide that.

Only our system will increase global affordability to levels that make dreams come true.

All other parties will have to engage at one point in austerity measures, but I ask you if it is a human-body how can it grow without food or with recycling which austerity measures are about? It's like removing food and proteins from one area of the body to another; overall growth is marginal, and this is exactly what has been happening for the past seventy years.

Ladies and gentlemen, the world requires bold thinkers and bold minds and I think everyone can have all that but it takes a lot of convincing and throughout I have gone to lengths to do just that and without doubt you can see clearly now that no other plan so far as growth to new heights is concerned can beat our system and plan.

Only Tomorrow's World Order has all the answers.

A holistic approach to global governance, financial and fiscal management, political system management and government and a new way that is fit for purpose in the provision of global peace.

You might be hesitant but revisit all the benefits mentioned above and come to the same conclusion as me that there is no alternative or a political plan that will near ours in all areas. If you are serious about real change and global wealth, national wealth and individual wealth then join us today.

VOTE TOMORROW'S WORLD ORDER

Solving global problems today giving everyone a brighter future and a say in things that matter to them;

Free health for all with the government getting the insurance itself and you getting another new savings account.

Tax-free income of your hard-earned money.

On average if you earn for argument's sake say $20 000 per year and you work from age 24 when most leave university until retirement around 65 years old.

That means you have worked for 41 years.

Assuming a rate around 22% of income tax you pay around $4000 per year as tax and a further $2000 in national insurance. Assuming this to be correct in 41 years means you pay; $6000 per year for every $20 000 you earn multiplied by 41 years. All your life you pay a whopping $246 000 as taxes and national insurance.

Now imagine the value you get from the government for that money. Pathetic! I agree.

We believe it is better if this money is put in your savings account and the government uses the account and the balance as collateral to provide free health cover, loans, pension, etc. How does that sound?

All our policies and methods have you as a central and important piece of the puzzle.

Imagine the banks stealing from you without you noticing embezzling small amounts in terms of Payment Protect Insurance. Imagine when you lost your job and only to be told that the insurance would not cover and is therefore useless and the banks then refusing to refund and pay you. Now imagine finding out that this was a pre-planned scheme to gather money as capital by the banks in order to invest in cryptocurrency the very time that bitcoin started after the 2008 financial crisis in 2011. Now imagine the banks have earned $billions in profits. It is true that a $2000 invested in 2010 in bitcoin would have made a whopping $2million in profits.

It gets interesting but still gross.

Now imagine the chances of banks making mistakes that affect millions of customers and a whopping $40 billion in deducted PPI monies.

Now imagine the possibilities of banks with the most educated people failing to follow their own rules of issuing the PPI and other loans.

Now imagine the regulating bodies like the Financial Conduct

Authority siding with 'thieves' in banks. Ask yourself if the CEO of a bank does the same thing stealing in small amounts over years and the chances when this comes out to get away with embezzling?

Now imagine governments bailing-out the banks making you lose everything.

Now imagine the governments using the banks to invest to raise money for political purposes and the names of all defaulters being passed onto the government by banks.

Now imagine a system when the government illegally hacks and tag all loans and mortgages defaulters and hold them to ransom through hacking and all getting tortured with some radiation being passed onto them as lab rats?

Now sit down and see justice in all that?

Is there justice I ask you?

Now breathe and picture a system that drags banks to court.

A system that protects your savings and fences your wealth that only you have access to.

Now picture a system that makes all the taxes and national insurance money you pay all your life be yours at the end when you need the money the most.

I can already see a smile on your face, and it does not stop there.

Imagine when you fall ill not having to pay anything or losing your savings or your wealth.

Imagine your kids and relatives enjoying your hard-earned wealth?

Imagine still owning your first house and giving that to your kids.

Imagine owning a lot of property and wealth? A situation where your wealth keeps increasing.

Now imagine a brand-new city from stretch with everything in it brand new; new railways, new clean cars that are electricity propelled and powered.

Now imagine everything new and clean fresh air and also imagine your grandfather insisting on staying in the old city and you laughing at his thinking failing to see the point but also seeing that everlasting smile on his face.

Imagine two worlds a brand new one and an old one all existing side by side with everyone choosing where to live with those who can afford to move to the brand-new city, etc.

Imagine where everyone can buy anything at the market value.

Imagine competition and how much can research, and development bring us; new flying-fast and safe means of transport, etc.

Imagine people living forever as you as they can in abled bodies having to enjoy their wealth at a young age when their bodies permit.

Imagine the quality of life improving greatly over the years.

Now relax.

Pinch yourself.

I tell you this is real and in reach, all you have to do is to;

VOTE FOR TOMORROW'S WORLD ORDER.

Your Future Your Say.

Signed 06 November 2019

David Gomadza

Founder, President, and the Global Party Leader

of

Tomorrow's World Order.

info@tomorrowsworldorder.com

00447745900178

www.tomorrowsworldorder.com

 The future belongs to the brave.

Are you in?

JOIN US TODAY!

Your Future Your Say.

THANK YOU

THE END

8 OTHER BOOKS BY DAVID GOMADZA

a. <u>Tomorrow's World Order</u>

b. <u>The New Laws</u>

c. <u>The New Single Reserve Global Currency: FutureGoldCoin</u>

d. <u>Fortified: Defensive Training: Training to Build Massive Walls Around Vital Organs.</u>

ABOUT myself: DAVID GOMADZA

I am the Founder and President of Tomorrow's World Order a political party that is to revolutionize global governance and the way countries are governed introducing a completely new system throughout the world with the aim of eradicating all global problems. I strongly believe that the current system collapsed many years ago and only a new system will solve today's global problems. A new thinking. A new way of doing things; taking wealth levels to new heights and changing the world forever.
I am ready. Are you?